# THE
# MATRIX
# FOR
# LIFE

*Pathways to Contentment*

RAJU HAJELA, SUE NEWTON,
KAYLIE RODRIGUEZ, MIKE DAVIES

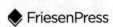 FriesenPress

One Printers Way
Altona, MB R0G 0B0
Canada

www.friesenpress.com

ISBN
978-1-03-911516-3 (Hardcover)
978-1-03-911515-6 (Paperback)
978-1-03-911517-0 (eBook)

*1. BODY, MIND & SPIRIT, HEALING*

Distributed to the trade by The Ingram Book Company

# Table of Contents

*as modified by Narcotics Anonymous

# Matrix Framework

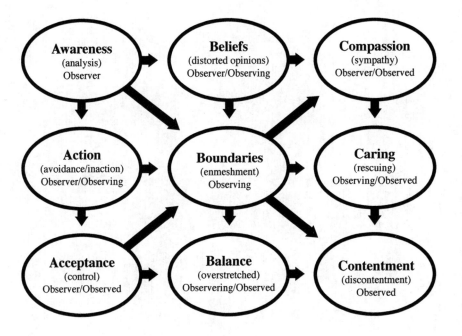

# Introduction

Life is an experience. How you experience your life is dependent on a lot of factors, such as your heritage, interests, and vocation. Yet there are commonalities that everyone shares, such as wanting happiness, peace, and prosperity to be the best that they can be. A lot of people get attached to material wealth, power, and status as a source of happiness; however, our experience as healthcare providers tells us that ultimately, contentment with what we have in life is a more desirable goal. The chase for "more," or feeling that what you have is never enough, or the pursuit of some arbitrary measurement of doing enough or having enough can be a trap. This is the source of a lot of misery for a lot of people.

In this book, we will use a 3x3 table or "matrix," which is like a road map from awareness to contentment. Awareness is the beginning, or the seed for everything. It has unlimited potential, as the more we are aware, the more our experiences expand in breadth and depth. We will discuss how you can explore and navigate each of the spaces in the matrix in various directions to arrive at the outcome: contentment. The journey from awareness to contentment also requires a process, which in the matrix is boundaries, or remembering what is within your purview for action and what is not. The plant or tree that grows from the seed is the process that results in the outcome of flowers, fruits, and more seeds!

In the matrix, action and caring are aligned with boundaries as part of the process, as are beliefs and balance. They form the central cross of the process that is essential, with awareness as the starting point and compassion and acceptance as intermediary outcomes, which ultimately all lead to contentment.

Compassion and acceptance become seeds for contentment, even though they are the fruits of awareness! Boundaries are at the core of the matrix. When we have healthy boundaries, we can enhance our experience of contentment, together with growth towards acceptance and compassion.

## 3x3 Matrix Framework

| Awareness | Beliefs | Compassion |
|-----------|---------|------------|
| Action | Boundaries | Caring |
| Acceptance | Balance | Contentment |

You may be wondering why we are focusing on a 3x3 matrix. We use it as a working framework, but the more profound reason is embedded in the nature of our existence. Many cultures around the world have this idea that we are all one, and things usually happen in threes. Have you ever wondered if there is a common thread for all humanity that is related to this? The short answer is yes! The long answer involves getting familiar with the knowledge contained in the Ved or Veda, which is the root of ancient knowledge and wisdom.

"Ved," in the ancient language of Sanskrit, is translatable in English as "knowledge." Sanskrit is considered the root of many languages around the world, even though its origins and current practice are largely associated with India. So, it is not surprising that the Ved is the root of knowledge and wisdom in cultures around the world. The Vedic construct, at its root, holds that unity or oneness is the source that always gives rise to three.

As humans, we can look at our physical, psychological, and spiritual parts as three parts that make us one (each individual). As much as our physical part has a genetic basis, our fundamental values (spirituality) guide how we think and feel (psychology), which then connects to how we behave and present physically. This idea of threes always starts with an idea or seed, which then goes through a process to lead to an outcome. Consider an idea or seed as the observer, being in the process as observing, and the outcome of the idea and process will be the observed. The Ved postulates that ultimately all is one—the observer. Without an observer, the process of observing and the outcome of being observed don't occur. As well, both are subjective and unique to the observer and are influenced by all the concepts discussed in the matrix.

***Observer***: Someone who watches or notices something.
***Observing***: The process of noticing/perceiving and registering an object with your senses.
***Observed***: Something that is observed, seen, or noted as an object or outcome.

The Vedic framework states that at a fundamental level, all the complexities and diversity in our universe follow this process of threes. In the writing of this book, the authors take the role of the observer, which through the process of writing, will have an outcome—the book—for us (authors) and you. You, the reader or listener, will be the observer, going through the process of observing and reflecting to reach more awareness (outcome) to motivate you to examine your beliefs and take some action. We hope that ultimately this will help you engage with life with renewed, expanded awareness and be more aligned with contentment.

Even modern-day physics has come to appreciate that the process of observing something changes the observer and the observed. For example, if you think of driving to a store to get bread, your awareness (observer) of needing bread (observed) initiates the process (observing) of driving to the store and purchasing the item; thus, the one gives rise to three, and hopefully you are content with the purchase. Psycho-behaviourally, interacting with any other changes both. Whenever we spend time with someone and share thoughts and feelings, we both come away from that interaction different from who we were before. The process of writing this book has allowed us four authors to have a much better appreciation of each other, and all of us have grown through the experience of honing our expertise and familiarity with the concepts that we talk about with our patients every day.

This book is an invitation to look at this idea of things happening in threes, in a 3x3 matrix, where each row can represent the observer—observing—observed, as can each column. The top left corner of this matrix is awareness, which is the starting point, and the bottom right corner is contentment, which is what we have come to appreciate as the ultimate that any of us can reach and enjoy over our lifetime.

So, the journey from awareness to contentment is what we hope you, the reader/listener/observer, can reflect on and enjoy, not just by reading about it, but also by learning to apply it in your own life by observing how it all plays out and sharing it with others. Shared observations about the observed from different perspectives of observing enrich the observers and the observed. This verifies how the observer and observed affect each other through the process of observing. This is exemplified by the famous thought experiment regarding Schrödinger's cat, which involved a cat in a box that could be alive or dead—it is undetermined until the observation actually takes place!

Ayurved, the health/natural medicine aspect of the Ved, follows the same patterns. "Ayur" in Sanskrit means life or lifespan. Ayurved thus refers to the knowledge of life over a lifespan. A fundamental tenet in Ayurved is that to be healthy means aligning yourselves internally and externally with your environment. The primary cause of disease is considered to be an imbalance or misalignment of a person's brain and body with natural processes within the universe. In Sanskrit, this misalignment is called *pragyaparadha*. This is simply translated as a mistake or misuse of our intellect. It refers to mistakes that we unknowingly or knowingly (yet minimizing the risk) make that results in us becoming unhealthy and unhappy in the long run. The fundamental mistake is to consider ourselves as being separate from everyone and everything else. Thus, the mistake of the intellect leads to actions that create imbalances in our body and/or mind. This leads to manifestation of diseases through dysfunction in our physiology, which can be verified intuitively in every one of us, since a healthy, functioning body-brain requires all organ systems to be working harmoniously within their own boundaries. Cancer, a common disease amongst us humans today, occurs often when one group of "abnormal" cells take over the normal cells in a particular part of the body and/or disseminate to other areas of the body, thus interfering with the healthy functioning of various organ systems, ultimately disrupting the body as a whole, resulting in death with multiple organ failure.

All diseases and dysfunction in humans are a reflection of the natural processes being out of balance. Some examples are overeating, eating when we're not hungry, and not being aware of the true needs of our body. Other examples include long-term, excessive use of substances such as alcohol, tobacco, and marijuana, and not exercising regularly, the detrimental physiological impacts of a sedentary life. A common way *pragyaparadha* happens is when our senses and mind make decisions without discrimination and these decisions are made without the use of our true intellect or wisdom. Decisions we make in life that violate the principles of natural and harmonious living lead to consequences over time. The most serious impairment is to the intellect of the observer, which compounds over a lifetime if remedial action is not taken.

The dysfunctional interaction of our five senses with the environment is called *asatmya indriyartha samyoga* in Ayurved, which can be translated in English as "untruthful interaction of the senses." So, if our touch, hearing, vision, taste, and smell senses get attached to harmful things without us realizing the harm, it leads to chronic imbalance and dysfunction that gets compounded over our lifetime with limited or no awareness that harm is occurring. A common example is a smoker saying that they like smoking, when in fact each inhalation brings harmful chemicals into their lungs, let alone the cumulative harm that occurs over the years. We can get truly attached to the belief and experience of liking the taste. The interaction of our senses with objects in our environment is the observing quality within the framework. It must be appreciated that a lack of awareness in the observer will result in dysfunction in the observing process, which in turn creates problems in the observed outcomes. We have briefly illustrated that in brackets in the matrix at the beginning of this book and will discuss it further in each of the chapters.

The manifestations of disease, the observed qualities, are called *kala parinama*, which in English translates as "consequences of time-space." For example, type 2 diabetes is a result of complex factors that manifest as the body physiology changes over time, such that the cells become impaired in healthy glucose transport with the help of insulin. The vulnerability is genetic, but what the individual (observer) does to live life in accordance with that or not, usually an unhealthy diet and lack of exercise (observing), determines the manifestation of diabetes (observed) in later life.

Another example is exposure to viruses, toxins, and infections that can enter your bodies at any given time. If you are healthy, with a functional immune system (observer), the manifestation of an infection or illness (observing) is determined by your body's ability to deal with these threats and the outcome of being asymptomatic, developing symptoms, or getting sick, which sometimes is fatal (observed).

All treatments in any system of medicine or healthcare around the world really offer support to the body-brain complex to bring it back in alignment by correcting a physical, chemical, or mental (awareness/thinking/feeling) injury or illness such that the natural forces within your body-brain come back into the best alignment possible given your genetic blueprint. Even with surgical treatments, the surgeon only sets things in alignment physically, and the body has to heal naturally, with some assistance from physical therapies and medications. Each person heals differently due to their own physiology in context of genetics and their environment. The high degree of variability amongst humans also reflects the diversity in manifestation. There is great variability in expression of natural traits and modifications of them through complex environmental interactions.

Holistic treatment acknowledges and appreciates that addressing the observer and observing qualities is an essential part of treatment rather than just trying to modify or fix the manifestations, symptoms, and signs of the disease. Treatment of any disease is better served if we can look at the beliefs (observer) and behaviours (observing) that are part of the disease and illness experience for an individual. Getting to wellness requires you to deal with the observer and observing qualities that can move you towards health, even in the presence of disease. For example, the primary chronic disease of addiction cannot be cured or fixed, but through holistic treatment and recovery you can enjoy a high level of wellness while being mindful of the disease within. As health professionals, we often discuss aspects of being (observer), becoming (observing), and belonging (observed) qualities with our patients on their healing journeys regardless of the seriousness or complexity of their diseases.

The Vedic idea of looking at the three qualities in everything around you is helpful in transformation of your awareness and consciousness. Although it is not something we will explicitly discuss in this book, you can explore the Ayurvedic body types of *vata* (movement), *pitta* (metabolism), and *kapha* (structure) in the same way. The body physiology aspects associated with *vata* represent the observer qualities that connect with the observed, *kapha* aspects, or structure of the body/brain, through the process of observing, which represent *pitta*, or metabolism. Very simply, you can see how air circulation in the lungs, blood circulation in your arteries and veins, and your gastrointestinal system moving the food through your body is the essential beginning part of your physiology. Metabolism is the processing of air, water, and food to keep you alive and functioning, which is all associated with *pitta*. All of this contributes to maintenance of healthy structure of all organ systems and your skeleton/muscle structure that are part of the *kapha* aspects in your body/brain.

Our five senses are also divided up in three: touch and hearing being part of *vata* (movement), vision being part of *pitta* (metabolism), and smell and taste being part of *kapha* (structure). If we are not aware, it seems odd that vision is metabolism; whereas if we understand that what we see is dependent upon the healthy processing of so many external inputs and internal processing, very similar to digital cameras and imaging techniques such as CT (computerized tomography), MRI (magnetic resonance imaging) and PET (photon emission tomography) scans. We often do not see what is in front of us; rather we are influenced heavily by what we believe about whatever is in front of us.

Even the sciences of physics, chemistry, and biology as a whole can be viewed as observer, observing, and observed, as biology is a derivative of physics through chemistry. The structure of the human body (biology) is maintained over a lifetime through myriad electro-chemical processes (chemistry) that require incredible and consistent awareness, energy, and consciousness of the observer (physics).

So, onwards to awareness!

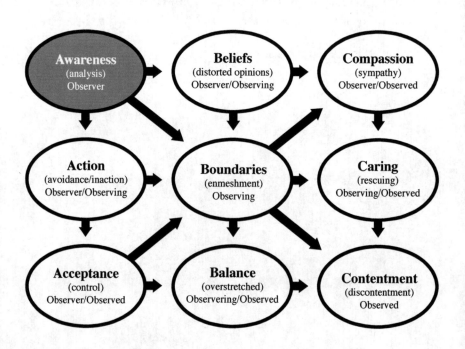

# Chapter 1: Awareness

*"Awareness is the greatest agent for change."*

*-Eckhart Tolle*

Why is awareness important? Awareness is a starting point: the core foundation for personal growth, health, and healing. Without awareness, we do not have the necessary insight to take action that best suits our needs. Awareness or consciousness is the ability to perceive, feel, and become conscious of events, objects, thoughts, and emotions. When things emerge in our consciousness, we become aware, although we do not necessarily understand what it is that we have become aware of. For example, we may become aware that we have a strong reaction to an event but not understand what we are feeling unless we do further exploration.

We become more aware when we learn to become more observant about ourselves and our surroundings. Then we can live purposely in the moment rather than being preoccupied with the past or future. When we are observant, we will begin to notice more in our outer and inner world. Some examples are when we drive a Jeep and we start to notice all the other Jeeps on the road (external), or we feel anxious and notice that there is tightness or heaviness in our chest (internal). Awareness allows us to recognize that we are not what we do, what we say, what we think, or even what we feel. While these things may define our experience of life, they do not define who we are. To be the observer is to witness this for ourselves.

Being self-aware is one of the most vital and fundamental skills of existence. Without self-awareness, our thoughts, feelings, and behavioural patterns are controlled entirely by unconscious beliefs, assumptions, and instincts. When we lack self-awareness, we create our own suffering and perpetuate it in the lives of others, creating endless pain and chaos. However, when we learn to become conscious of unhealthy thought patterns, core beliefs, ideals, assumptions, and choices, we learn to pause, become more mindful, and not believe everything our mind is telling us. This enables us to become more peaceful, loving, and intelligent human beings.

Awareness of the effects of past experiences in our present-day life is essential in taking responsibility for ourselves, just as awareness of our future aspirations guides what we may or may not want to do in the present. In many ways, the future is the observer quality, where there is pure potential. We can leverage that to re-examine our past (observed quality) to get a new perspective in living (observing) today. Misalignment can result in a lot of sadness, blame, rumination, and recrimination about the past, such that we can be overwhelmed with anger and stress in the present while living in a lot of fear about the future.

### Self-awareness

Who am I? This is truly an open-ended question rather than a defined destination, as you are constantly changing as you live your life. Self-awareness is the capacity to be introspective, to better understand your needs, values, and what gives you meaning and purpose in life. Awareness of yourself allows you to connect with your true self and spirituality, which really refers to your relationship with yourself and the rest of the universe. The more you know about yourself, the easier it is to be proactive rather than reactive, to adapt to life changes and challenges, and to eventually find contentment through the processes we will discuss in this book.

Talking openly and honestly with others and getting valuable feedback from others is essential to increase self-awareness, as we all have "blind spots" that we may be unable to see while others can. These blind spots are part of our "blind self," which is what is known about someone by others, but is unknown to the person. This blind area can also be referred to as ignorance about yourself, or issues in which you may be deluded, which refers to fixed beliefs that are not necessarily connected to reality. By seeking and getting feedback from others who have more objectivity, you can open up the blind pane in your life and thereby increase yourselves-awareness through open-mindedness. This does not mean that you blindly follow someone else's views but rather examine your own awareness or perspectives in context of what others may offer as another way of looking at the issues. Sadly, a lot of strife results when people try to change others' perspectives rather than appreciating all of them such that they can find the commonalities that provide true direction. If you are scientifically minded, you may well know that many data points may look chaotic. Yet if you find the mathematical equation that represents those manifestations, you can plot a nice graph that represents variables that explain the realities of what is happening!

Over time, self-awareness can evolve from understanding the nature of the self/identity, in context of the specifics of your life to understanding the nature of the self in context of the spiritual essence of who you truly are. People often have a very concrete experience of attachment to their physical existence that may or may not have a spiritual aspect and shift to appreciating that they are spiritual beings that have a physical (human) existence. With enough reflections, discussions, and growing awareness, it becomes apparent that our minds are very complex and really abstract in their ability to perceive various aspects of our physical existence and non-physical thoughts, feelings and imagination. It becomes humbling to come to appreciate that even with the powerful capacities and complexities of our intellect, with its perceptions, with our five senses and the sixth sense of intuition, we can only understand small fragments of reality. Furthermore, it also becomes apparent that who we "think" we are is not truly who or what we are.

### Awareness of thoughts

It is common to equate active mental dialogue related to what you may think about yourselves internally, changing negative to positive, to being mentally healthy; but this is a gross misunderstanding. You are not your thoughts, and your thoughts do not always accurately represent who you may be, have been, or want to be!

Typically, people average about six thousand thoughts a day; most are repetitive thought patterns which are habitually repeated to yourself. It is necessary to have awareness of your inner dialogue or thoughts and recognize your thoughts aren't necessarily a reflection of reality. You can start listening to the voice in your head as more of an observer with some distance rather than attachment or analysis of whatever may be playing out.

It helps to pay particular attention to any repetitive thought patterns that have been playing in your head, perhaps for many years, that you have come to believe as truth about yourself when in fact they may be related to some problem in your brain that could be genetic or environmentally programmed. If you can listen to that voice more impartially rather than getting caught up in it, believing it to be true, you can shift perspective. Even if you don't get a different perspective by yourself, an opportunity arises to discuss it with others to see if others may or may not experience something similar.

Think about a time when you've experienced a thought but not taken it seriously. For example, maybe it was when you were riding your bike one day and a car cut you off, so you nearly had an accident. You thought about catching up with the driver and giving them an earful about their reckless driving. You immediately saw how crazy that thought was, and you did not act on the thought; rather, you let it go, realizing the thought was not worth taking seriously. If you did not take the time to reflect, you may have got into a verbal altercation that made the problem worse rather than better. In an extreme form, you can get stuck in delusional thoughts related to all car drivers being against cyclists and assuming that the driver may have done it on purpose. This can easily turn into more paranoia and fear that can get generalized in other aspects of your life.

We all have the ability to recognize that a thought is just a thought, and that we do not have to take it seriously, buy into it, or indulge it. Just because something pops into your mind does not make it something that you need to act upon or believe in. It is not who you are. It's not reflective of the type of person you are, either; it doesn't make you a good person or a bad person. We can't control or stop our thoughts, but we can choose to not engage in them and take it to the level of speech or action. Consider that a thought is just a thought. It is the awareness or the observer quality of what it actually means in a bigger context that allows us to choose what we do with it rather than being enslaved into automatic action or reactivity because of it.

When we hang onto thoughts and ruminate, the thoughts can start to snowball. We start to place judgment on them, taking them too seriously, and life becomes heavy. This is commonly referred to as "making a mountain out of a molehill." When thoughts become exaggerated and blown out of proportion, that then impacts our perception of an event and takes us away from reality temporarily, or, over time, more permanently, as we become bitter and fixed in our perceptions and ruminations.

So, what is the difference between thinking and awareness? Thinking is when your mind creates thoughts about the situation you are in. Awareness is when your attention is focused on the situation, simply observing with your senses. You are aware through what you see, hear, feel, smell, and taste. Thinking separates us from the immediacy of the situation, and it is always in the context of the past or future. It is affected by what we may have experienced in similar circumstances in the past and/or what we may want to see happen in the future. Invariably, it interferes with our perceptions and colours our reality. Awareness, on the other hand, gives us a direct perception of the situation and allows us to perceive it more accurately. It can also provide us with an opportunity to check things out with others if we do not get too attached to our perceptions as being the only truth.

A simple definition of thinking is the action of using your mind to produce ideas, decisions, memories—the activity of thinking about something. Typically, we place opinions or judgment on our thoughts, whether we realize this or not. Our thoughts are impacted by our environment, culture, family, and time period. For example, we might think it is rude for a person to text us rather than pick up the phone and talk in person. Almost immediately we make a judgment and opinion about that person based on our own thoughts. Awareness is learning to be present or pay simple attention in the moment without judgement.

A great tool to increase awareness is meditation. When we practice meditation, the goal is not to become thoughtless. It is to become more aware; aware of our thoughts, feelings, sensations, and our surroundings without judgment or attachment, letting them come and go without jumping up to record them and/or do something about them. Those who meditate regularly will naturally develop more self-awareness over time, as that simple practice, usually twenty minutes twice daily, can help our brain act better in its observer capacity with awareness rather than judgement and analysis throughout our day quite naturally. By being still and present, and focusing internally, we have greater capacity to take stock of our feelings, thoughts, and physical sensations, which is not possible when we are busy, distracted, and focused externally on the world around us.

### Awareness of feelings

It is not uncommon for people to become disconnected and numbed from their emotions if they are continually focused and engaged in their thinking. Becoming aware of core emotions and feelings as they surface without coping mechanisms can be disconcerting. Emotional awareness and processing are key for the psychological component of health and well-being. Feelings and emotions are commonly used interchangeably; however, there are distinct differences between the two. Becoming aware of both feelings and emotions helps change our unhealthy behaviours and how we deal with life. Emotions are internal physiological responses that may be conscious or unconscious; our brain creates biochemical reactions altering our physical state. Emotional reactions can vary individually but are generally universal and instinctual. For example, we can feel terror when we perceive a bear attack. We feel happy when the sun is shining on a warm summer day. Feelings are sparked by our emotions but then coloured by our personal experience, beliefs, and memories.

It can happen in reverse as well, and feelings related to the emotion of fear can trigger an emotional and physical fear response. It is important to gain awareness of our emotions and feelings, as they play a significant role in how we interact with the world around us. If we live in perpetual fear of the future, our feelings, emotions, and behaviour will become a reflection of this and adversely impact connection with others. If we feel content and happy, keeping our emotions and feelings in perspective, our behaviour and interactions with others will be significantly different.

By increasing awareness of emotions and feelings, we can then become more mindful of our thoughts and actions and how we choose to react and experience the world. Being able to do this will make the difference between a calm or chaotic life. A chaotic life and discontent go together, whereas cultivation of an orderly, calm, and balanced life leads to more contentment.

Another gift of self-awareness is to accept feelings for what they are. Too often, when we identify with our feelings too strongly, we begin to get lost in them rather than viewing them objectively, without judgement. Alternatively, avoidance of emotions and feelings in an effort to numb and escape will eventually lead to acting out in unhealthy ways as a means to escape the emotional turmoil. All the unprocessed and unrealized emotions eventually catch up with us and come out as painful, or what can feel like overwhelming and unmanageable, feelings. It is essential to have emotional awareness, so emotions move from the unconscious to the conscious level for health and wellbeing. Once we have identified feelings, it is then necessary to work towards (action) to ultimately accept those feelings.

The first level of emotional awareness is knowing when feelings are present in ourselves. We become aware of the feeling when we first perceive it. It is common, though, that we may think about it rather than just staying with the awareness of what we may feel at that moment. We may not know exactly what the feeling is, but if we notice and acknowledge that we have some feeling(s), we are developing emotional awareness. Feelings act like a barometer to get our attention; they are neither good nor bad, they just give us information, and they let us know when we are out of balance. After acknowledging a feeling, it is helpful to identify it, as the more we can do this, the easier it will be to take appropriate action. It is good to get into a daily habit of asking yourself "how or what am I feeling?" as too often we are too busy doing and thinking, which leads to becoming disconnected from our emotions and feelings. It is important to feel the feelings rather than think about feelings.

Some of us are naturally more inclined to thinking, so we can become avoiders of feelings, whereas others may be feelers who then get confused and overwhelmed with trying to impose thinking on the feelings. Following acknowledgement of feelings comes processing and then acceptance of them. Too often people attach meaning to feelings that makes them "good" or "bad" and not appreciating that there is no "right" or "wrong" when it comes to feelings. So, the challenge is to look objectively at feelings and recognize them as information or messages. A concept that people often struggle with is "there is no such thing as a bad feeling." It might feel bad, but it is just a feeling like all others, and we need to pay attention to what it is telling us. Just because something feels bad does not make it a bad thing!

It is not uncommon for people to avoid strong emotions that are typically perceived as "wrong" or "bad." Stuffing of emotions can lead to rage, anger, and violent outbursts that can do a lot of internal damage over time and of course create confusion in relationships externally. Often these feelings may appear to come "from nowhere" but are really rooted in "emotional constipation" that has been building for some time. This is often connected to shame and a variety of other emotions. Fear, anger, and shame are three core emotions that all humans experience during their lifetime, and it is vital to gain more awareness of the people, places, and things that trigger these emotions. Without this awareness, people instead typically do the same thing over and over again or blame others for their problems, which per-petuates self-pity or being a victim.

Fear is a natural, powerful, and primitive human emotion. It involves a universal biochemical response as well as a variable individual emotional response. Fear alerts us to the presence of danger or the threat of harm, whether that danger is physical or psychological. Sometimes our fear response stems from real threats, but all too often it can also originate from an imagined danger or threat. An example of this is the fear of judgement from others or fear of public speaking, which may be connected to shame and the perception of not feeling good enough. It is important to be aware of our fear response and consider if this is False Evidence Appearing Real (F.E.A.R). A fear response is also connected to worrying and being anxious about something in the future. This can lead to a desire to control the outcome rather than letting what will be, be. It's good to have awareness that the more we try to control/fight/avoid fear (or other feelings too), the more they build up and eventually overwhelm us like a tidal wave.

Anger informs us when we have been violated in some way; when our needs are not being met or an internal or external boundary has been crossed. Many people are socialized and/or grow up in households where anger is not an acceptable emotion to express. People then suppress their anger and do not learn how to express it in a healthy way, often leading to increased reactivity, inappropriate outbursts, or rage. As with all feelings, anger is not good or bad; it is just information. All of us need to pay attention or be aware when we feel anger so we can deal with it in a healthy way, such as talking about it in an assertive versus aggressive manner. Physical activity, journaling, and finding some solitude or alone time to decompress are all healthier ways to dissipate anger and/or observe the information those feelings are provid-ing. As with all feelings, the key is being aware of them. Without focus on awareness, the risk increases to want to escape, numb, or seek relief with substances and/or behaviours, such as eating for comfort rather than hunger or blaming others for our problems.

Shame is the emotion related to the feelings associated with "I am bad." It is an intensely painful and uncomfortable emotion, and when people feel shame, they feel unworthy, a sense of failure, and like they are not good enough. Shame is an emotion experienced by everyone at some point in their lives, and it is a reflection of beliefs about oneself that impacts confidence, esteem, and worth. Shame is often connected to expectations that you may carry or perceive are being placed on you by people in your life. It is often connected to regrets from the past, i.e., "shoulda, coulda, woulda," which creates symptoms of depression, such as feeling worthless or useless, hopeless, and lacking motivation for any action.

Fear has an observer quality to it, as it is abstract in terms of a real or imagined threat. Anger has an observing quality to it, as it is usually related to something you have done or someone else has done. Shame is the observed or the manifest emotion that you can get stuck in related to the past. Feelings of guilt say, "I did bad" versus shame, which says, "I *am* bad." Hence, fear is a common experience for people that often manifests as anxiety, whereas people will often deny anger, commonly experienced as resentments or blaming others. Shame is the hardest to acknowledge, as people will often cover it up by being proud of something while avoiding talking about the truth of what they may be feeling. Awareness of all feelings is the starting point before you can appreciate the different aspects of yourself that they represent.

Some recommendations to increase awareness include the following:

### Find solitude on a daily basis

It is common to use "busyness" as a way of escaping our feelings, especially when the feelings are bad or overwhelming. Many people chronically feel the need to "do something" when often the best way to truly experience and appreciate life is to be still with ourselves, do nothing, and just be!

In order to develop self-awareness, it is important that you start with an "empty canvas," and silent solitude is the best place to start. This is because solitude grounds you in reality, and although it can feel scary and lonely at first, spending time alone each day provides you the opportunity to reflect on yourself, what you have done, what you have said, what you feel, and what you would like to do. Solitude realigns you with your deepest needs and desires in life and is thus a perfect conduit of self-awareness. Some examples of silent solitude include going for a walk or hike in nature, sitting on the grass in the park and listening to the birds, or sitting by the fireplace in your living room.

### Contemplation, Concentration, Meditation

Nowadays, there are many techniques available to help you learn how to slow down your mind and body, as this is helpful to becoming more conscious of the inner chatter within you that often goes unnoticed. Consider practicing some techniques daily as part of your routine. For more information about contemplation, concentration, and meditation, please see Appendix A.

### Keep a daily private journal

Recording all your thoughts in a safe and secure place helps you to not only track yourselves-growth progress, but also helps you to be more authentic with yourself. When you are honest about your thoughts and feelings and when you find a place to express them, they no longer stay bottled up in your mind, which tends to create a lot of tension and stress. Writing your thoughts down gives you an opportunity to explore and reflect on what you truly think and feel, and what you can do to feel better or remedy certain issues. You might like to write out these thoughts in a private place, such as a journal; or write them out and then destroy them shortly afterwards.

Which of these activities appeal to you?



Which of these activities are you willing to do?



What are you doing now, and how is it affecting your awareness?

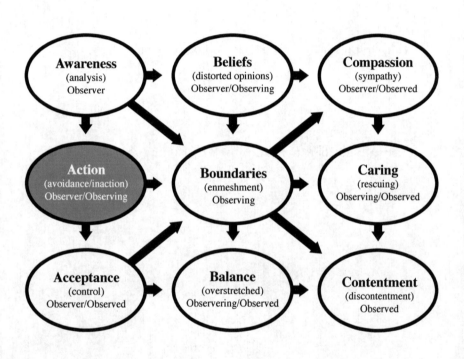

# Chapter 2: Action

*"Words may inspire, but only action creates change."*

*-Simon Sinek*

Without action, we are not engaged in the process. By remaining in the seat of knowing without doing, we become a bystander in our own life. We are complacent and stagnant. This state of inertia, as described in physics, leaves us in a resting state of existence unless that state is changed by an external force. Awareness alone will not produce change. The state of knowing is not enough. If nothing changes, nothing changes. So, where do we begin?

What is action? Simply put, action is a verb, a word that represents process. It is fluid and moving. Action refers to the "doing" that allows us to keep moving one foot in front of the other. The key in action is to ensure we are "being" rather than just "doing" by checking off the boxes of task completion. What this means is that connecting to "being" allows us the space to consider how the action feels, connects, and relates to our value system. Is this congruent with our truth?

Action is not synonymous with motivation. Often, we may fall into the trap that we need to feel motivated to act. We cannot think ourselves into acting. It is the action itself that creates and cultivates motivation. As an action is undertaken, the thinking will catch up and action flows with an ease. We can act our way into healthier thinking!

In the matrix, as action follows awareness, it is driven by some clarity and insights; some knowledge that action is required. This places us in the observing category as movement flows towards acceptance (observed). However, action can also be in the role of observer and create new awareness as it is undertaken. This is represented in the column view where awareness, action, and acceptance can all be observer qualities, reinforcing the strength of the observer as we become familiar with the process of observer, observing, and observed from the row perspective. Boundaries naturally follow as the observing role, resulting in caring, compassion, and contentment as the observed role as is evident in the column view in the matrix.

Some people commonly describe themselves as a "go with the flow" type of person. This easy-going persona may be a disguise for avoidance and can take place at a subconscious level. This person may not be connected to themselves, or may not have awareness of what their wants, needs, and boundaries are. Or perhaps they are riddled with fear and shame that keeps them in complacency. They may be influenced by the messages around them. Some people may find they flow with these messages without much thought or consideration about how they truly feel. This easygoing mask likely covers up those who are avoidant and/or disconnected from their own feelings and truth.

When external forces impact us when we are in a disconnected state, we tend to feel powerless and potentially victimized. It feels like things are happening to us. Typically, resentments build, leading to feeling further disempowerment and victimization. This commonly results in a lot of complaining, more feeding into the cycle of self-pity, looking for sympathy, and wanting others to rescue, thus becoming more and more entrenched in a state of inertia or inaction.

Action allows us to take on an active role in observing the process so we can really consider how we feel. True harmony exists when congruence occurs from within ourselves to the world outside of ourselves. Connecting to this harmony requires action, as the world is fluid and constantly moving around us. Without considering ourself holistically in the process, our actions become misguided and misplaced, resulting in more confusion and dysfunction.

As discussed previously, awareness will bring clarity within. As this clarity grows, you may recognize an incongruence with your own physical (biological), psychological, social, and spiritual realms. This incongruence will create feelings that may be uncomfortable. These feelings are messages that change is necessary. Without acting, this discomfort will escalate, and disharmony will increase. The challenge is that action initially may also be uncomfortable. People are vulnerable to staying stuck in the "same old same old" because the discomfort of it is familiar and predictable. There is a sense of resignation and hopelessness in context of the emotion of fear, where you stay trapped in the familiar discomfort rather than considering action that may be a venture into the unfamiliar, which generates unfamiliar fears and other feelings that one may be avoiding and/or unwilling to face.

Full awareness, however, is not necessary to create action. What is needed is *some* awareness and willingness. The impulse for action is some willingness. People often wait to get motivated to take action, but it is really willingness, even in the absence of motivation, that breaks the inertia. Motivation is more a thinking function, which can be a trap, whereas willingness is more a feeling related to exploring something different. Action can create space to allow you to see through a different lens, and in turn, awareness can grow. This new action can create a space that allows for new learning to develop. As an example, you may find that you are hearing the same messages or suggestions from those around you. You do not necessarily see the benefit in that particular action, but in time you decide you are willing to try it out and see what happens. As this action occurs, you may experience a moment of "Oh! I understand now!" and new learning occurs. Through the process of self-awareness, awareness of thoughts and feelings, you can explore being through a holistic lens—biological, psychological, social, and spiritual. Action can occur in each of these areas.

## *Biological action*

This is directed to your physical health. Having awareness around your physical health can provide opportunities of where action may be needed. Consider the basic fuel source of self care: food intake, hydration, and sleep. "If you do not put gas in the car, it will not be able to go anywhere." Food, water, and sleep are the necessary components for our body to function. Action can look like an exploration of food nutrition and hydration of the body. You may not be aware of what your food and water intake looks like. By taking action and drawing attention to what you are eating and drinking and how often in the day, more specific action can result. You may begin to explore, "How does it feel to drink eight cups of water in a day?" This results in information and awareness. Or alternatively, you may have awareness that increased water intake is needed for your health and take action to increase water intake a cup a day. Regardless of what is driving this action, connecting to how this feels for you is essential.

Biological action also means providing attention to sleep patterns. Having consistency is an important aspect of sleep hygiene. Going to bed and waking up at the same time is helpful. Reducing electronic exposure and limiting screen time, especially close to bedtime, is essential. Introducing stretching, breathing, mindfulness, and meditation are all avenues you can take to enhance quality of sleep. However, sleep hygiene is not the only aspect of healthy quality of sleep. Sleep challenges are often a symptom of disconnection from yourself. Incorporating action to connect to yourself within the day will have a direct influence on sleeping patterns. Journaling before bedtime, if you are having difficulties falling asleep, and/or journaling if you wake up early are great ways to increase awareness of your feelings and repetitive thoughts that are usually related to analysis or problem-solving.

Exercise is another component of biological health. This does not mean you need to start training for a marathon! If exercise is something new for you, starting with a twenty-minute walk three times a week is helpful; if that sounds like too much, starting with ten minutes is all right. Being specific in your commitment is important, though, as this enhances the likelihood of follow-through. Start wherever you are willing rather than trying to motivate yourself to something that may look too challenging initially. The idea of doing things gradually and with attention is essential for developing healthier exercise routines. Consulting someone who knows more about it is also helpful in getting to action and feeling supported in continuing action.

*Explore.* What does physical self-care look like for you in the domains of:

Food intake, water intake, sleep patterns, and exercise patterns?

With what you have written down, what are you applying action to currently?

## *Psychological action*

This pertains to your thinking patterns and feelings. As mentioned, thinking is the action of your mind to produce ideas, decisions, and memories—the activity of thinking about something. However, it is important to remember that your thought patterns can be misleading and will provide you with misinformation at times. You can be caught up in the busyness of life around you such that you are disconnected within. The first place of action is carving out space to tune inwards. Ensure you have a quiet space, a pen, and a piece of paper. From here, you can begin to write. This is the action that is needed to increase awareness, and it leads to more acceptance of what is rather than getting stuck in what "should be, would be, could be ... only if ...what if ..."

There are no rules when it comes to journaling. You may simply start with putting out on paper what thoughts are flowing in your mind. As you release what is on your mind without judgment, you may notice certain themes, words, or patterns that are coming up in your writing. Perhaps there is extreme language such as "always, never, everyone, every time, everywhere, good, bad, success, failure, right, wrong." All these words are very black and white. This action of journaling can lead to further action in terms of exploring thoughts and feelings with others professionally and/or through mutual support. Perhaps it is an opportunity to practice internal boundaries of removing those words from your vocabulary and replacing them with alternatives. Or perhaps it may look like reframing the sentences in your journal where these words come up. As an example, "This was an absolute failure" can over time be replaced with "This was a growth opportunity that I learned from!" An active tool of asking yourself "What would I say to someone else in the same position?" can help you provide yourself with a shift in perspective.

Underneath all thinking are emotions and feelings. Emotions usually exist at a subconscious level while we are busy thinking our way through life. Whether they come up to a feeling-based conscious level or not, we still carry emotional energy with us. These emotions will bubble up unpredictably into our current reality if left unchecked and unexamined. Through actions such as journaling, meditating, and sharing with others, our emotions can be connected to and be felt at the conscious level. This "feeling of feelings" allows acknowledgement, connection, and release of the emotional energy that we all carry at all times. The question to ask yourself is "how am I feeling and what is this telling me?" rather than trying to analyze or thinking "why am I feeling this?" It is encouraged to move away from the "why" questions, as this leaves you in the thinking state and removes you from the feeling state. When you are caught up in the "analysis paralysis" of thinking, you lose the capacity to connect to feeling.

Sometimes the action of doing nothing provides a space to release feelings. By sitting with your feelings and holding space for them, it allows feelings to flow through rather than being repressed and/or actively suppressed. Acknowledging what feelings exist and drawing attention to where in the body these feelings are being felt can place you in the more active state of observing that also strengthens the observer with more awareness.

*Explore.* Create a space and time in your day to sit for fifteen minutes and journal. Write down specifics of when and where.

Ask yourself "How am I feeling?" and write down whatever comes up for you.

What is a triggering person, place, thing, or situation? What thoughts are generated? What feelings are coming up? Can you reframe your thinking patterns? Writing down a few thoughts and feelings here can serve as a seed to write more in your journal.

### Social action

This is a very important area of holistic self-care, as none of us exist without a social context of our upbringing, choice of vocation, and communities that we are aligned with. As self-awareness is cultivated, you can begin to look at who you do or do not surround yourself with. The role of congruence provides you with insight as to the health of your social circles. As explored previously in the chapter on awareness, you gain clarity over your own values, needs, and wants. First, do you act in accordance with your own values? If you do not, you are likely living your life inauthentically and may not be fully aware of it. This is often driven by the feelings of shame and fear. There is fear around what other people will think of you. Will other people reject you if you express more of your authentic self? The irony is that it is you who is rejecting your authentic self if that is happening. The act of embracing your own authentic self leads to an honest display of who you are. In turn, others can see you for your true self and real, vulnerable connections can develop. Taking action in this area then leads to healthier social connections with like-minded people focused on exploring life honestly, rather than unhealthy traps where social interactions reinforce dysfunction, often with gossip, one-upmanship, and putting others down. This can be very difficult to step out of because of the familiarity and stuckness that grows over time.

Do the people you connect with have similar values to you? If not, you will likely feel some inauthenticity or guardedness in those relationships. This incongruence and discomfort can cause you to isolate and avoid people in general. Alternatively, the awareness of incongruence can generate some willingness to look at establishing new connections and supports.

There is also the concept of introverted versus extroverted personalities. These personality concepts refer to how an individual will reenergize. An introvert will reenergize in a space with themselves while an extrovert will feel reenergized when around other people. Both personality types experience fear and shame in a social context. However, an introvert is vulnerable to isolate, which we call "act-in," whereas an extrovert is vulnerable to distract and hide amongst other people or "act-out." Both types are vulnerable to blowing up when the pressure just keeps building over time. Fundamentally, self-awareness of exploring your motivation in interactions (or lack thereof) is essential. If you are looking for distraction, escape, avoidance, or validation, consider this a trap. Usually, you may not get exactly what you are looking for, and that creates conflict and strife, whereas at other times you may get what you are looking for, which in turn makes you dependent on getting more of it. Invariably, this leads to dissatisfaction, as "more" can never be sustained forever and you experience withdrawal when the body/brain does not get what it has become used to getting.

*Explore.* Do the relationships around you mirror your value system?

What is your motivation in spending time with yourself? With others?

## Spiritual action

This is a very subjective and personal process. It is important to appreciate that spirituality is not synonymous with religion. Religion refers to a set of rules, rituals, organized beliefs, and practices that is shared within a community. Spirituality is an individual practice that connects you to something greater than yourself. It is personal and can be unique to you. Spirituality is exploring your own method of seeking and expressing meaning and purpose. It is the experience of your connectedness to the present moment, self, others, and the universe around you. Religion can be a vehicle for your spirituality if you can develop a personal connection; however, it can become a trap if it feeds people-pleasing and/or image-management that are common amongst religious communities around the world.

If spirituality is something you have not explored before, how do you learn how to connect spiritually? This process is not an intellectual process; it is experiential. Through taking a form of action and exploring with an open mind, experiences will naturally occur. Those moments of feeling grounded, connected, peaceful, serene, and present are indicators of a spiritual presence. Some common avenues of spiritual practice include meditation.

Through this practice you become more aware, present, and connected to your thoughts, feelings, and surroundings. Meditation creates the ability to be present and self-aware in your experiences rather than distracted and preoccupied. It helps clarify what may provide meaning to your life, and it leads to better awareness of your values rather than trying to live up to someone else's values in a social realm by seeking approval and/or fearing disapproval.

*Explore.* What are your values? Are you acting in accordance with your values? Are you trying to live up to someone else's values or an image that is projected by someone else?

The act of prayer is another common spiritual tool. It is intentional communication to something beyond us. It does not have to incorporate folding your hands or kneeling. It is an action that can occur anywhere and anytime. There is an element of acknowledging your feelings and releasing them by putting them out there (to the universe, God, higher power, nature, etc.). Creating a daily gratitude practice is an avenue of action that builds spiritual health. Connecting to and acknowledging experiences within and around you that you are thankful for daily creates a powerful shift in perspective. Faith and trust build as you become more grounded and present. Welcoming in gratitude, especially in times of great challenges in our lives, is a testament to spiritual health.

*Explore.* Start your day with a prayer. If you are unsure of how to pray, thank the universe for your day and ask for guidance on how to show up throughout your day.

At the end of your day, write down three things that you are grateful for.

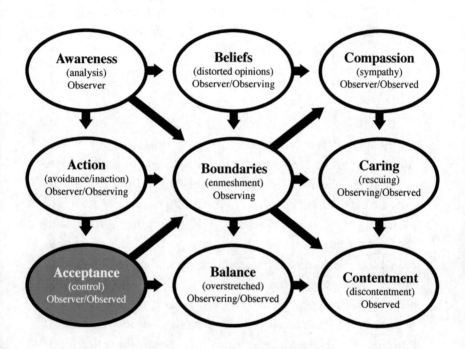

# Chapter 3: Acceptance

*"God, grant me the serenity to accept the things I cannot*
*change, the courage to change the things I can,*
*and the wisdom to know the difference."*

*-Reinhold Niebuhr*

Human experience generally occurs in five holistic components
or levels: the physical, mental, emotional, social, and spiritual. These are also referred to as the biological, psychological
(mental and emotional), social, and spiritual aspects of self, as
mentioned previously. As already discussed, the spiritual level
is often misunderstood and confused with organized religion.
This tends to make accessing spirituality difficult for those who
identify as atheist or agnostic. The concepts of spirituality and
organized religion are in fact separate, and are different on many
levels, especially if we appreciate that spirituality is personal,
whereas religion often requires social conformity in accord with
certain norms established by the organization. Religion may be
a vehicle for spirituality, but often becomes over-focused on a
prescribed social order. Behold, as an example, the peoples of the
North American plains. These cultures existed for thousands of
years without contact from the outside world, without written
language, without any doctrine, and their knowledge and ways
of knowing were passed down generation to generation by song,
ceremony, story, and through story robes, which are the closest
thing to written language they had. Story robes are essentially
pieces of art painted on dried and stretched animal skins

depicting the culture's history through time, going back to their very beginnings.

This is relevant to acceptance because contained within these teachings are what can be called spiritual teachings or spiritual principles that are quite universal. From ten thousand years ago to modern times, from Blackfoot to Buddhist, these same principles exist in all recorded human cultures through time, regardless of geography. These principal teachings are an essential design for healthy living, for living comfortably with ourselves and with others in our social communities, all in context of acceptance of what is. They tell us to live in congruence with our personal values and beliefs, as well as with those values and beliefs of our communities. They remind us that we must practice the virtues of faith, trust, truth, honesty, respect, integrity, patience, tolerance, understanding, humility, compassion, empathy, love, gratitude, and the principle that is the focus of this chapter: acceptance. They form a structure that is the observed quality in our matrix, but they also serve as guidance for the observer to move through life. The spiritual principles reflect the connection to the universe described in the Ved.

So, what is acceptance? Within the constructs of the matrix, acceptance is the observed outcome of the journey from awareness to action. It is also the beginning or observer state along the journey from balance on the road towards contentment.

Acceptance is an acquired skill and an art. It is often difficult for people, as our brains generate thoughts and feelings that can create the trap of giving primacy to our own thoughts and feelings as being correct, such that we want what we want and push to get it rather than looking at acceptance of what is while adjusting our wants and needs in context. As is true for any skill or art, it must be practiced consistently and with intentionality for us to become proficient. It is said that it takes a minimum of ten thousand hours to achieve mastery over a skill or art, and even when we have achieved mastery, we must continue the same dedication to practice over time that led to the mastery in order to maintain that level of skill. Even masters make mistakes, as there's simply no such thing as perfection. According to the Jedi Master Yoda, "The greatest teacher, failure is." The more we practice acceptance, the easier it gets; though often the circumstances in which we are practicing acceptance remain hard, the practice can make them feel manageable. Lack of acceptance feeds unmanageability, fueling conflict that can be very destructive and devastating over time.

Acceptance is also an experience, a mindset, an attitude, a way of being congruent with health and wellness. It has the observer quality that can lead to more balance and contentment, but first and foremost it is the outcome, an observed quality from expanding awareness and consistent action related to skill development in practicing the art of living. At the experiential level, acceptance is consenting to receive something that is being offered either physically, mentally, emotionally, socially, spiritually, or holistically. At the mindset or attitude level, acceptance is the person's appreciation of the reality of a situation, their recognition of a process without attempting to change or protest it. Who among us has not used the saying "it is what it is" in an effort to move on with or get through a situation that is beyond our control? This phrase has perhaps been used more than at other times in recent memory because of the viral pandemic.

Radical acceptance, where we simply accept everything as it comes, is offered in a variety of cultures and philosophies in various ways. Some interpret that as becoming a passive observer versus an active participant in our own journey. Our understanding of this concept can be challenging, as we may perceive it as a bit like rolling over and playing dead, being a doormat for others or perhaps life itself to walk all over us. In contrast, the Vedic concept suggests active participation in observing rather than control or passivity. The Serenity Prayer, as presented at the beginning of this chapter, focuses on the recognition of things we cannot change, which is truly a healthier way to navigate life with acceptance. We are not always offered choices in so many things that can potentially influence the pace and direction of our lives that are beyond our control. Further, it is important to be mindful that while we get a say in what choices we make, as presented in the second part of the Serenity Prayer, in terms of things we can change, we don't necessarily get a say in how those choices will turn out. In the context of outcomes, the ultimate authority will always be the universe, which is a fundamental spiritual construct that recognizes that the laws of nature that govern the realm in which we exist are always supreme.

Many people find connection with the idea of a higher power that is more personal, which may be expressed in religious terms if one so chooses. As much as we can have hope that things will turn out a certain way, what happens will be determined by a power greater than ourselves, as there are always other variables that we cannot foresee because of the limitations of each of our own personal perspectives. It will be what it will be, it is what it is, in concert with the functioning of the universe—that is what acceptance is ultimately about. Connecting with others and some sense of perspectives other than your own takes you to serenity, courage, and wisdom.

It is so important to appreciate that there is an inverse relationship between acceptance and control—actively or passively—by avoidance. As illustrated in the Serenity Prayer, there are times when we do have the ability to change things, to make choices that may influence events, yet that choice does not mean control. There are also many instances where we are simply powerless over what is happening in our lives. Humankind's struggles with powerlessness are vast and numerous throughout our history, as unforeseeable forces have determined the rise and fall of empires and civilizations. If we each look at our own lives, we can see the many devastating effects of our stubborn refusal to see what is; or our blindness to the truth that is in front of us as often pointed out by others who have a different perspective; or our outright denial in terms of being powerless over people, places, and things. In these instances, it is often our own brains that become our biggest adversaries.

Our brains generate so many thoughts that we experience through what is best termed ourselves-talk. Through self-talk, our brains create stories, fantasies, and misperceptions that have the potential to mislead us. These stories, fantasies, and distortions are compounded by our thinking styles and by our feelings. Thinking styles such as minimizing, catastrophizing, all-or-nothing thinking, and wanting instant results while putting in minimal effort, in combination with the feelings of shame, guilt, fear, anger, and resentment, are blended together, distorting our perceptions of reality. These distortions exacerbate our motives, intentions, and perceptions. We lose sight of what is real and true. This manifests in the belief that we can control circumstances and situations which we are in fact powerless over, thus taking us in a direction opposite to acceptance, which can fill our lives with more conflict, both internally and externally.

It is during these challenging times that acceptance becomes of critical importance. Surrendering to a power greater than ourselves, God as we understood him/her/it, or the forces of the universe, when we recognize our powerlessness, frees up our time and our energy from trying to change and control what we cannot. Letting go of trying to control, rescue, or fix the impossible allows us to focus on what is possible, to focus on being who you are, on how you are feeling, and to focus on what you need to do in order to deal with the reality of the situation. Acceptance means letting go of control and allowing the space to become clear on our feelings, needs, and boundaries. With acceptance, we can acknowledge what is true and make healthy decisions.

A helpful red flag or warning sign that we are indeed practicing non-acceptance is the presence of decision-based evidence-making, which is of course the opposite of evidence-based decision-making. In undertaking decision-based evidence-making, we have already decided what is true, and our brain becomes busy manufacturing the evidence in our minds, based on our misperceptions, to make our distorted perceptions be the reality that we project. For example, we have already decided our spouse doesn't love us enough, so we then look for evidence to prove this, such as them not listening to us, or spending more time at work or with friends. Invariably, this leads to conflict and confusion for the individual engaging in decision-based evidence-making and those around them.

The practice of non-acceptance, to not surrender to the things that are beyond our control, means we are fighting an unwinnable fight, waging an unwinnable war. We get stuck in a quagmire of wasting our time, our energy, and our efforts. We become enmeshed in any number of forms of crazy-making, generating unmanageability in our lives, potentially creating enemies and greatly diminishing ourselves in the process. The universe has a way of course-correcting itself, and in these cases, will present barriers and consequences that are intended as signs, as evidence that we are on an unhealthy path. When we are practicing connection to spiritual principles, we are more likely to notice and acknowledge when we deviate onto the unhealthy path and change directions. When we are in non-acceptance, we will push harder, fight harder, try to control harder. The barriers and consequences will continue to come, progressively getting bigger until we ultimately are forced to make corrections from a place of major crisis. What is needed in these moments is surrender. With awareness and action, acceptance becomes possible.

The word surrender conjures many feelings and thoughts, not the least of which is that of failure or defeat. This may give rise to other feelings such as weakness or shame. However, in truth, the path to freedom from suffering, release from pain to inner peace, also called contentment, runs through laying down our arms to stop fighting that which cannot be defeated. It is through acceptance that we are able to surrender and find liberation. To reach acceptance, however, one must move through the myriad of feelings that exist in the emotional realm; feelings such as anger, frustration, shame, not-good-enough, self-pity, sadness, loss, fear, guilt, and resentment. The way through fear is to have trust and faith. The way through shame is to practice compassion and serenity. In the realm of resentments, the way out is through acceptance, sometimes in the form of forgiveness.

The concept of forgiveness is often misunderstood and itself has some negative connotations associated with it, such as if you forgive the person, place, or thing that has wronged you, you are somehow weak. It may feel like you are saying it was okay to hurt you, and that forgiveness is for their benefit. The reality is forgiveness represents strength from the perspective of acceptance. It means you are making a choice not to dwell in the past, but rather to live in the present moment. It does not necessarily mean forgetting what happened, but rather, remembering what happened to be in the past, and not have it continue to colour the present and future potential. Most importantly, forgiveness is not for them, it is for you. It is the way you let go of the pain you alone are carrying. It is the way to move forward in health. Letting go of resentments and learning how to move through feelings puts you on a path of acceptance of circumstances, of others, and most importantly, of yourself. It is for this reason some choose "remember and accept" with appropriate boundaries that may be necessary to prevent future harm.

It is important to explore acceptance across the spectrum of your life. This includes looking at all your relationships, such as those with your parents, siblings, children, intimate partners, friends, and extended family; with your work, your time, your money, the future, the past, the present, your body, your feelings, and your relationship with the universe, or if you like, a power greater than yourself. That being said, our most important relationship is the one we have with ourselves. Consider that we project an energy at all times, through our attitude, mood and behaviours. We often attract back what we project out. The quality of your relationship with yourself will, to a large extent, determine the quality of your relationships with others, and with the world. It is important to ask yourself "How do I truly feel about myself? Do I like myself?" If the answer is unclear, or the answer is no, it indicates some work or action needs to be taken. Chances are that feelings such as shame and guilt or perhaps fear and anger need to be explored to work our way to acceptance. Unresolved feelings generate emotional pain that is often expressed in self-talk, thus affecting your relationship with ourselves. This can manifest as chronic pain, depression, and anxiety. Addiction involving substances and unhealthy behaviours is a common denominator, as the disease itself leaves you handicapped in dealing with feelings in a healthy manner. Hence, treatment and recovery focus so much on learning how to identify and process feelings, with the help of others, as a brain with addiction lacks the capacity to do it by itself.

It is important to keep exploring where we are resisting acceptance of what is, as this will show us where we are hanging on versus letting go, where we are still trying to control what cannot be controlled. As we move towards acceptance, we move towards acknowledging how we feel, what is happening, and what is true vs. what is false. We move away from avoidance and move towards action. If we take a page from the twelve-step world of Alcoholics Anonymous and other related groups, it tells us that we need to pause for reflection before we act, that we need to turn to others for support rather than trying to manage things on our own, and that we would be best served to turn towards spirituality and positivity rather than focusing on the negatives; in doing this, we ultimately connect to our authentic selves better. As we do that more and more, naturally we find ourselves moving towards contentment and health.

Here are some questions to reflect upon when exploring your current level of acceptance:

*Explore.* In what areas of your life are you struggling with acceptance?

Who are you? What are your values? What are your needs? What gives meaning to your life?

What does powerlessness mean to you?

What things are you trying to control that are beyond your control?

Can you focus on what you feel right now rather than trying to change your feelings and/or get stuck on analysis of why you feel this way?

When reviewing the first column of the matrix, Awareness, Action, and Acceptance together comprise an observer quality. Thus, the "A" column all together reinforces the observer qualities in the matrix, even though separately, awareness is observer, action is observing, and acceptance is observed. The process of awareness, action, and acceptance act as one observer quality and can separate out as three or collapse back into one. This is an amazing experience once you get the hang of it. It is highly beneficial to consciously explore this in your day-to-day interactions, which can give amazing perspective of the big picture (forest) when you feel trapped in some nagging problem (a tree).

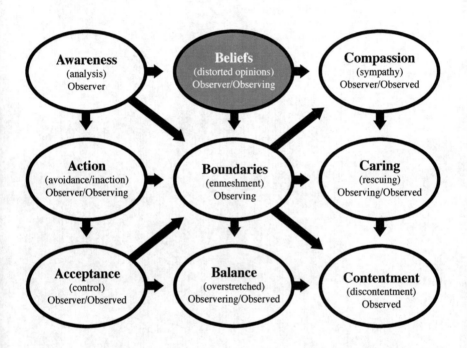

# Chapter 4: Beliefs

*"Our greatest ability as humans is not to change the
world; but to change ourselves."*

*-Mahatma Gandhi*

Beliefs drive our day-to-day choices and interactions with others
in ways that we may or may not be fully conscious of. They have
an observer quality to them; they are the lens through which we
perceive our world around us. They also have an observing quality
to them, as they filter awareness through which other ideas
such as compassion are derived. Giving compassion high value
requires a belief in it before we can experience it. For example,
our awareness tells us that our world is hierarchical and competi-
tive. "Survival of the fittest" is a common belief that arises out of
that. But how that survival happens for each one of us depends
on many factors. How do we become part of the fittest rather
than being eliminated? What does being eliminated mean?
These ideas take us to the core of our existence: our beliefs about
life and death. Do we believe that all beings have a right to exist,
regardless of their status? Do we believe in honouring others'
feelings or act in ways to ensure our own dominance?

Our beliefs affect what we see and how we see it. Beliefs also
take us towards answering the question of why something happens
or doesn't happen. Religious beliefs are common guideposts for a
multitude of humans on our planet as a vehicle to experience spirituality, a connection to the rest of the universe. There are others
who shun religious beliefs and have their own individual or shared

collective belief system that guides their day-to-day living choices. We often do not see the world as it is but rather see it as we are.

We often use words such as confidence, ambition, passion, inspiration, self-esteem, and motivation to describe whether we believe we can do something or not. At the core, all these ideas connect with what our beliefs are about ourselves and others. Some people may be stuck in a set of beliefs that say they are worthless and/or action in a particular direction that they think is futile. They would remain stuck until some changes happen in their beliefs. As represented in the matrix, changing beliefs require growth in awareness as a fundamental step. Taking the column approach says that we have to go through cycles of awareness-action-acceptance, which allow us to explore what entrenched beliefs we may have that drive us in directions that may or may not be beneficial to ourselves and/or others.

Beliefs about health, disease, and illness are central to whether we take action to deal with our problems and how we do or do not address them. Health and disease refer to the physiological experience within the body. Illness and wellness refer to our perception and experience. We can experience any combination of the four. For example, we can have disease present, yet experience wellness; and on the flipside we can have health and experience illness. The goal is to move to both health and wellness. Beliefs are what keep people trapped in the familiar even when it is harmful, rather than exploring the unfamiliar but healthier ways of living. Getting started in unfamiliar directions requires us to challenge our beliefs, an exercise that is very difficult if not impossible to do effectively alone. We require others with more expertise and/or lived experience to trust and rely on to guide us through the unfamiliar until it becomes familiar, which means changing beliefs.

There is a dominant human behaviour theory called the health belief model (HBM) that basically says that human beings choose various behaviours, primarily what is healthy, on the basis of their beliefs. Hence, changing behaviour requires changing beliefs. One major assumption in this is that choice capacity is unhindered in all of us. One pitfall in HBM is that it does not recognize that all humans do not have the same brain capacity, hence, variability in behaviour often occurs by personal choice (high self-efficacy) or by a lot of direction (low self-efficacy). Further, certain aspects of mental health dysfunction, especially with the disease of addiction, may make us believe that there is capacity to make a choice, for example, in maintaining control. Yet if these are things that we have impaired control over, or no control over, then the choice doesn't really exist. It takes repeated trials and errors sometimes for individuals to come to terms with what may or may not be possible because of certain talents, interests, or mental capacity we may or may not have. For example, music and art come easy to some people whereas they are difficult for others. So, we may hold beliefs that something is hard or easy when in reality it only applies to us or others similar to us.

Believing one thing and doing another generates a lot of shame in people and actually becomes more and more of an obstacle. Hence, beliefs have to be clarified to see what actions or behaviours we may be engaging in or may be happening due to dysfunctional beliefs. We do not necessarily have to change all beliefs, especially when some may be too deep rooted in brain function or social culture; however, it is essential for all of us to come to terms with which beliefs need to be left alone and which ones require action to move in a healthier direction. The chapter on boundaries will explore in more depth how to have boundaries around our own beliefs and others' beliefs.

So, how do we get to know our beliefs? It requires a lot of self-reflection, journaling, and talking. In today's world, with social media, the algorithms that provide the daily feed are built around our beliefs on the basis of our behaviour and what we access on the internet. Hence, we can check out our beliefs daily and unfortunately get reinforced by the same beliefs, which leads to a lot of conflicts with those who may have different beliefs and are just as strongly reinforced with their daily feed. The healthier approach is to clarify all beliefs—yours and others—without judgement. Sometimes we may discover that many cultural beliefs around the world are so contradictory that it is hard to fathom what to believe. At other times we may find consistent beliefs across cultures that are perhaps more universal.

What about beliefs about our interests, passions, and abilities? Most of us are passionate about music that we like, but we may or may not have the talent or training to play an instrument. Just believing that we can be an accomplished musician does not necessarily make us one. Rather, believing we are better than we are and/or better than others may represent dysfunctional thinking that is called grandiosity. So, a belief can take us in particular directions but also trap us if that belief is not based in reality.

What are your beliefs?


What is the evidence for these beliefs?

What is happening to you and those around you and what do you see/hear/feel that is connected with these beliefs?

Have you considered that it is a big challenge for any of us to see the world as it truly is? Partly, we are constrained by our senses and brain function, but largely we are limited by our language of experience and constructs that we have acquired through our learning through education and experiences. We hope you can continue to consider how we see the world more as we are. The old adage "seeing is believing" would be more accurate as "believing is seeing!"

One of the most popular behaviour therapies in our world today is called cognitive behavioural therapy (CBT). One of its pillars is to recognize how some distorted beliefs, rooted in thinking or cognition, may be contributing to the persistence of unhealthy behaviours. Hence, changing behaviour requires changing beliefs. This sometimes gets translated as changing thinking, which at most times is actually not possible. Our brain does not recognize the difference between "think this" or "don't think this," and often gets stuck in analysis about why we may be thinking whatever we are thinking. It is important to appreciate that if the focus is kept on challenging our beliefs and appreciating other people's beliefs—clear or distorted—a gradual shift toward clarity starts to happen in our own thinking. As discussed in previous chapters, underneath thinking are feelings that sometimes are difficult to even articulate, and underneath that is our value system and what gives meaning to life. Therefore, it becomes critical to examine beliefs in the context of spiritual, feeling, and thinking perspectives.

The most profound aspect of recognizing that we see the world as we are is that as we learn and change, our beliefs shift and the world looks, feels, and sounds different! It becomes more wonderous! In the matrix, beliefs are the process through which awareness grows, resulting in compassion for all that is. We can all have our likes and dislikes, but it is important to appreciate that there is a trap in falling prey to the belief that something is inherently good or bad. True harmony results from appreciating yourself and others and being free to express yourselves without forcing a particular set of beliefs on everyone.

It is also important to appreciate that beliefs have an observer quality to them as the seed that can grow into boundaries, which honour you and others—a tree that can be part of a forest but maintain its identity. From the column perspective, that is how we get to the outcome of balance, which is a process, too, if we look at acceptance as the preceding window in the matrix to balance.

Beliefs thus have an observer and observing quality to them. The broader our appreciation of our beliefs, which may be similar or different than others, the more grounded in reality we become. We can celebrate where we may agree in our beliefs with others, and we can respect when beliefs differ and maintain curiosity and dialogue so that both parties can grow in that interaction without feeling forced to choose one over another.

Beliefs can come from empirical scientific observation and understanding of the nature of things. Historically, most people believed that the world was flat, or the Earth was the centre of the universe, yet as the evidence emerged about how Earth is a planet revolving around our sun, our beliefs shifted. The expansion of awareness through beliefs allows us to understand and explain so much more in relation to seasons, for example, that result from the movement of our planet around the sun in the course of 365/366 days. Even the appreciation of our planet revolving around its axis resulting in sunrise and sunset, moonrise and moonset, shifts the old beliefs about the sun and the moon disappearing and then reappearing.

It is most important to appreciate that beliefs can become objectified or fixed when we lose our ability to stay in process and be open to the process of expanding awareness. So many conflicts arise amongst us interpersonally and amongst nations around the world because of lack of appreciation of the variety of beliefs and conflict over who has the right or wrong beliefs.

It is so necessary to keep exploring our own beliefs to see if they serve us in a beneficial manner for growth or if they have become obstructive such that the flow of life and connection to the rest of the universe has become dysfunctional. This is not an easy process at the best of times, but especially difficult in a world where scientific and technological progress is challenging our world views. Newtonian physics, as a simple example, serves us well in the mechanical world we live in day to day; however, quantum physics and Einstein's general relativity theory have the world's greatest minds still working towards better understanding of our universe and harnessing forces for technological advances.

Consider the following questions to explore beliefs that are contrary to your current ones:

What beliefs do you dislike in others?

What is the evidence for their beliefs in contrast to yours?

What is your interaction and/or connection with people who have those beliefs?

As you engage in this exercise, hopefully clarity will emerge about how understanding and compassion can be the outcome of recognizing others with different beliefs because of their culture, experience, and/or education. You can get a better understanding of your own beliefs when you contrast them with others' beliefs without disparaging them.

Boundaries are the healthiest option to disengage from conflict when differences in beliefs is the heart of the conflict. This part is especially hard if you are used to sharing similar beliefs with others who you have been close to in the past when you may have changed, and they haven't. With attachment, there is a vulnerability or desire in trying to change them rather than respect them for where they are. It is important to trust that whatever their process may be, with its own consequences that may be harmful, yet change will only happen when s/he is ready, rather than being cajoled or forced by someone else.

What are your beliefs about compassion?

What are your beliefs about boundaries?

How do you communicate your beliefs with others?

How do you not communicate your beliefs with others?

What beliefs have you held dear forever?

What beliefs have changed for you?

What beliefs are you unsure of?

Who can you have an honest and open conversation with about beliefs?

None of the above questions have easy answers, and they may require a lot of exploration. In the field of addiction and mental health, a fundamental difference in belief about what addiction is drives the age-old debates about whether it is a disease. Or is it a behaviour problem? Are people addicted to particular substances? Or do they have the disease of addiction that manifests in myriad ways? Behaviours are certainly part of the disease of addiction, but our thesis, as presented in our previous publications, is that behaviours are not the disease nor are they the cause of the disease. They are manifestations of a disease that is biological, psychological, social, and spiritual at its roots, primarily driven by genetics and dysfunctional reward, motivation, memory, and related circuits. Many focus on just changing behaviours in relation to a particular substance or an unhealthy behaviour such as eating disorders or gambling. We offer a perspective of recognizing the underlying disease of brain function and focus on brain health, such that in recovery people learn to accept the things they cannot change and change the things they can with professional help and peer support. Thus, they accumulate wisdom to keep learning the difference. Appreciation of powerlessness requires surrender, where courageous action is needed to move out of the trap of avoidance, denial, rationalization, minimization and projection. Regardless of your beliefs, ongoing exploration of all angles is needed to navigate the complexities related to the disease of addiction or any other disease you or others may be dealing with.

Mental health problems are also often classified as behavioural disorders in the Diagnostic and Statistical Manual (DSM) of the American Psychiatric Association. Many of these behavioural disorders have overlapping signs and symptoms, so what is chosen as a diagnosis is dependent on what the professional believes. This is a primary reason why different practitioners can come to different diagnoses in the same person, given the same symptoms and signs. On the other hand, if we recognize that behaviour is a manifestation of the brain not working right and the focus shifts to what is actually happening in the brain with the classification, such as for addiction, being based on brain dysfunction, the beliefs in behaviourally based diagnoses can then be appreciated as misguided misinformation.

We posit that even with any serious disease, it is possible to move from illness towards wellness, which many recognize as a transition from "I" to "we" as we examine and explore our beliefs with others around us. Although the disease is a dysfunctional state of a characteristic form, illness and wellness are very personal experiences. Through personal reflections and talking about beliefs with others, we can get to compassion, appreciating others without attachment to wanting to change them, and creating boundaries to choose how much or how little interaction we may want with particular people, places, or things.

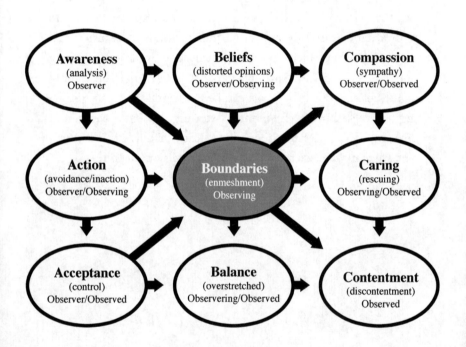

# Chapter 5: Boundaries

*"We are all bags of particles—both mind and body—and the physical facts about the particles can fully address how they interact and behave. But such facts, the particulate narrative, shed only monochrome light on the richly colored stories of how we humans navigate the complex worlds of thought, perception, and emotion."*

-Brian Greene (Physicist)

Boundaries define things by marking off one thing as being separate from another. Our universe is largely energy, as described by current understanding in physics. Yet, it is also made up of particles that make up everything from inorganic to organic matter, from gigantic stars to the most minute, microscopic entities of genetic material encased in protein coats that we call viruses.

Everything around us that we perceive through our senses fundamentally delineates bounds in terms of what we think, feel, touch, hear, see, taste and smell! Physics tells us that all matter is bound in accordance to some fundamental laws and forces energy into particles. These particles then manifest as protons, neutrons, and electrons: the fundamental building blocks of atoms. The atoms then come together to form molecules from the simplest H2O (water), which makes up the biggest part of us, to complex genetic material and its translational proteins inside all living organisms. It is quite amazing to think how simple, yet complex natural phenomena are that give rise to matter that we then define as organic (biologically active) and inorganic (not biologically reproducible) yet needed for biologic growth (e.g. minerals in soil for plants/trees and minerals in food for animals, including us humans). These organic and inorganic particles then organize themselves in accord with our DNA to manifest the human body and brain that we use to navigate through life, with some concept of "I" in our mind that is the perceiver or the knower.

What we perceive as sound is actually a set of frequencies that our ear and brain are able to translate as different tones. What we perceive as light is also a set of frequencies that our eyes and brain translate as specific colours. The vibrations that make frequencies of sound are just movements in air, just as the vibrations that delineate colours are light of different wavelengths. Every seed represents a defined blueprint for something to develop in accord with the natural processes that we do not control. Each of these things that we grasp with our minds is discrete because of a boundary that makes it discrete.

Boundaries are all around us and within us. Every single cell that makes up our body does its job to make the whole body and brain function well. We do experience threats from within (for example, cancer cells) and without (for example, infections resulting from bacteria or viruses that challenge our immune system to maintain boundaries and balance). There is an ongoing intricate dance that determines how we maintain health. Boundaries result from various active processes and are necessary to ensure the functioning of our universe as we know it around us and what we experience within us.

Every day we have countless thoughts and feelings streaming through our head, some from memories, some related to what may or may not be happening around us, and some originality whose source is hard to pin down. Can you imagine what would happen if we tried to follow all of them? So, choosing to focus on one idea while letting other ones go is essentially an example of internal boundaries that we all engage in all the time. Similarly, we have a choice every day regarding what we do or do not do, so choosing something to engage with, whether it is an activity or person, delineates a boundary.

Beliefs represent boundaries to some extent as we choose one idea over another. So, it makes sense that in the matrix, awareness that can be pretty unbounded, action that has some bounds, and beliefs that have more bounds all precede boundaries. Our beliefs determine how we are going to establish boundaries. For example, if you believe that sons should obey their fathers without question, then there is no boundary between father-son, as the son is just an extension of the father. This is common in our society where parents impose their ideas on their children so much that the children do not have an opportunity to choose for themselves and are often left floundering when put in a situation where a quick decision is required of them for themselves. On the other hand, if you believe that the parental responsibility is to help your child become independent, then boundaries are established incrementally to foster that sense of independence and identity.

In relationships, boundaries delineate what defines one person versus the other. Sometimes that delineation is unclear, so someone becomes more focused on another person rather than staying focused on their life. This is very common for mothers and fathers who will focus on their child more than anything else. We call that boundary blurring. This is detrimental to all people involved, even though it may feel good to some or all parties. As much as a father and a mother are individuals, sometimes, in an effort to be united in parenting rules, they can lose their identity as a person and the child is left to perceive them as a unified authority figure—parents. The child is left with limited choices in this situation, such as to either comply or rebel, often setting up an unhealthy child-parents conflict that may be perceived as a zero-sum game of winners and losers.

Boundary blurring can result in a situation where no one in the triad of father, mother, and child is able to develop or maintain their identity. In this dynamic, everyone wants the other to be a particular way, which can lead to an appearance of family togetherness, but the natural inclination for independence in every one of us would create tension, conflict, and resentments. Often siblings get thrown into a lot of chaos if parents pit one against another in trying to establish what an ideal child should be. In such a situation, as there is no understanding of personal boundaries, it is virtually impossible to even have a dialogue or discussion about how to deal with the problems as they arise or fester. So, problems and conflicts are usually avoided until the pressure becomes too much for everyone, resulting in a blow-up. This disruption can be followed by a regrouping and everyone trying harder to maintain appearances, such that the dysfunction festers even though things may be patched up on the surface. Alternatively, if each triad of father-mother-child maintains a healthy dialogue as each individual grows in their individual life journeys, with boundaries and encouraging autonomy, then healthier choices can be made for joint activities while allowing freedom to explore what they may wish in their own life, especially in areas where it has no direct impact on the other. If siblings and parents can celebrate their individual strengths and support each other in meaningful ways, the relationships become mutually supportive and benefit each individual and the whole family. Autonomy and mutual support encourage each to pursue their own potential for their optimum life and health rather than enmeshment, which can become a stranglehold of suffering while the family desperately tries to project an image of solidarity.

Boundaries establish limitations and parameters under which we can all operate. For example, licensing and regulatory bodies establish standards by which an operator or service provider delivers or conducts their business. Laws are established in societies, to which the population generally abides to ensure that everyone is equally respected and given latitude to function the best way they see fit within those boundaries. Laws are enforced to varying degrees to ensure societal functioning within certain parameters.

Trust is a central component of boundaries where there is a common understanding of what is desirable for healthy functioning. Years ago, one of the authors of this book (RH), developed an acronym for TRUST that has been used as a guide for group psychotherapy. TRUST = Truthfulness, Respect, Understand, Support, Transformation. This acronym reflects the essential qualities that are necessary for every individual to develop and grow to their optimum potential.

Healthy boundaries mean that each of us gets to know and focuses on who we are as individuals. Then each person can function with others in a manner that is harmonious and supportive to everyone around. This means that we must have a sense of healthy internal boundaries: what we choose to focus on and what we process and allow to pass through. None of us have the capacity to block thoughts and feelings; if we attempt to, it can produce blockages within—emotionally and intellectually—that may become visible at inopportune times and interfere with our lives. There is a misconception with some people, even in professional circles, that we can think our way into right action. The truth is that action requires willingness, honesty, open-mindedness, and commitment that has to be utilized even when thinking is not clear, which is common because of mixed-up feelings that we all experience at times. This is especially important for those who have addiction, which is a brain disease that generates distorted thoughts (addictive thinking) and a dysfunctional emotional response (primarily shame and fear, which often get expressed as anger and resentments). It is through healthier action that someone gets to healthier thinking and feeling. When we increase our capacity for healthier boundaries internally, this also means looking at boundaries externally.

We are all influenced by our social environment. We may not have a choice in who our biological family is, but we always have a choice in who is in our peer and social groups. Even with our biological family we can exercise choice in when and how we interact with someone depending on our awareness of how that interaction impacts us adversely. Does the relationship reinforce dysfunction, or is it beneficial and supports mutual growth?

Often, a dysfunctional environment is characterized by enmeshment, without boundaries or with blurred boundaries. In these situations, there is usually a lot of "shoulding" that goes on, interfering with our ability to deal with internal boundaries and "shoulding" that generates shame and/or analysis paralysis. There is often too much thinking about what is right and too much conflict generated in getting everyone to agree to something that they may not want to or be ready to agree to. Boundaries require each person to take responsibility for themselves and allow the other person(s) to be wherever they may be. It requires acceptance and compassion in relation to ourselves and others to give and take time and space for self-examination, expansion of awareness to move towards growth rather than choking in stagnation with various parties trying to control the others.

Our social interactions with others are essential for sharing thoughts and feelings, validation, and understanding for mutual support. Support is often offered in the form of sympathy, where people who have had similar experiences can commiserate with their feelings. Sympathy is dangerous ground, though, for boundary blurring. As much as there may be commonalities in feelings in relation to similar experiences, there is a vulnerability in people re-living their traumatic experiences repeatedly, such that enmeshment and trauma-bonding happens, which then leaves little room for processing, reframing, and growth. Trauma-bonding replays old scenarios that are usually fear and shame based, with generous sprinkling of resentments that can get people stuck in victimhood. This then is an invitation for rescuers who are not aware of their own boundaries and limitations to sweep in and fix. These same rescuers can also become perpetrators and/or feel victimized themselves as frustration continues to manifest all around when people are stuck. In these situations, lack of awareness limits healthy action and false beliefs create more enmeshment. Even though people may be well-meaning, lack of boundaries is a recipe for disaster.

Empathy, on the other hand, focuses on understanding ourselves and others while maintaining connection to ourselves rather than losing ourselves in the feelings and thoughts of someone else. It allows us to hold space for one another, to understand what they are feeling, to listen without judgment, while putting all things in perspective by focusing on what we can change rather than dwelling on what we cannot. It allows people to be true helpers and protectors in a supportive way without rescuing or fixing. Empathy with healthy boundaries helps people survive and thrive with providing inspiration to each other.

We hope people can see the integral link between action and boundaries to really appreciate the work that is required to establish and maintain boundaries. It is also important to see the connecting links with acceptance, such that the observer qualities that are enhanced with awareness and action as well are enhanced for the observing quality of boundaries. Compassion, balance, caring, and contentment, which will be discussed in further chapters, all flow through from boundaries. All the other eight matrix windows require boundaries, even though awareness is the most unbounded. It is important to appreciate that our awareness is limited by our capacity of perception, hence open-mindedness and healthy boundary-based interaction with others leads to more awareness and growth.

Interactions with virtually no boundaries have become commonplace in our world, especially on the internet these days, and this generates a lot of conflict. This is understandable, as we can either be too easily influenced or be too rigid in our beliefs, getting caught in projecting them onto others and making assumptions at times, with a lot of resentment and consternation when others are coming from similar levels of limitations. It is the ultimate way of not seeing the world as it is but getting caught in an echo chamber of reactivity related to who we may be as a result of our experiences. In the matrix, boundaries are the core observing quality from all directions!

What do your boundaries look like?

Internally?

Externally?

What areas require change internally?

What areas require change externally?

Who are the people externally who are reinforcing dysfunction?

What activities are reinforcing dysfunction?

Hearing?

Touch?

Vision (screen time)?

Taste?

Smell?

What activities are or would reinforce healthier thoughts, feelings, and behaviours?

Who are the people that can support healthier thoughts, feelings, and behaviours?

Much reflection will be needed to appreciate the centrality of boundaries in our existence and how necessary they are for us to be able to live a meaningful, contented life. Boundary blurring in thoughts, feelings, and relationships can create distortions, confusion, strife, conflict, and suffering. Conversely, being able to combine discrete ideas, people, and things in creative ways, while appreciating our boundaries, strengths, and vulnerabilities, leads to a healthier, more vibrant life.

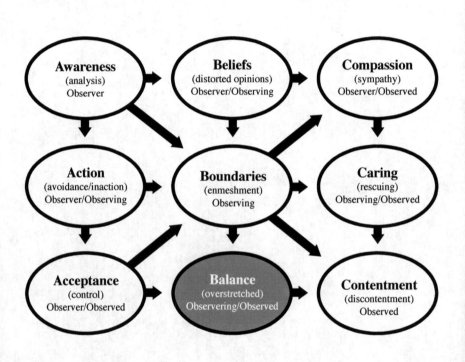

# Chapter 6: Balance

*"I've learned that you can't have everything and do everything at the same time."*

*-Oprah Winfrey*

In order to remain healthy, it is important that we live a balanced life. A balanced life means different things to different people; it will vary for everyone. Balance is often understood as taking appropriate action when circumstances dictate so as to maintain equilibrium, or as making all things equal and giving equal weight to all things, but this isn't always possible. Balance is also defined as a means of judging or deciding; a counterbalancing weight, force, or influence; or mental and emotional steadiness. Therefore, living a balanced life means determining what is most important to us and expending our time and energy accordingly.

Many people in today's society are busy and frequently over-committed. Productivity and busyness are celebrated and encouraged. We can feel less worthy and unimportant when we don't lead a "productive," full life all the time. In order to find balance in our lives, we need to appreciate the trap of thinking that more things, more commitments, more of everything, is better. "Enough" is often an elusive concept. What is enough? We all need to become aware of what it is that matters most to us and what is deserving of our time, energy, and resources and then make adjustments to our lives accordingly. Without self-awareness, having clarity of our beliefs and values, in terms of what gives us meaning in our lives, it's very challenging to find and maintain balance. Boundaries are a central aspect of finding balance, the observed quality that flows from the observing.

When we know what we want more of in our life, then we also have to commit to giving less in other areas. Finding balance comes from giving time and energy to the people, places, and things that foster passion, growth, meaning, and purpose, to name a few. Likewise, reducing or eliminating the people, places, and things that do not support overall health and well-being. Boundaries are required in order to have balance, and once boundaries are in place, balance can be attainable. To reiterate, balance will not look the same for everyone, therefore it is necessary not to compare yourselves with others. Finding your current and unique life balance simplifies your life in a way that brings freedom, peace of mind, and contentment.

When examining health and balance, we need to consider the bio-psycho-social-spiritual perspective, the components of holistic health that have been discussed in previous chapters. The biological or physical aspect of holistic health focuses on taking care of the physical body, which includes a healthy, balanced diet, adequate sleep, and regular exercise. Psychological or emotional health includes subjective well-being, perceived self-efficacy, autonomy, and self-actualization of our intellectual and emotional potential, acceptance and processing of all feelings, and consciously reframing self-talk to focus on gratitude, acceptance, and compassion, among others. The social aspect of health revolves around relationships with self and others. This dimension considers how we relate to others: how we connect, communicate, and get along with the people we are surrounded by. As we know, we need to have a healthy relationship with ourselves before we can have healthy relationships with others. If our lives are out of balance and we are disconnected from ourselves, it will be challenging to have authentic, meaningful relationships with others. Social connection with others is a vital part of life but can easily become off balance due to other priorities or issues such as mental health, chronic problems, and diseases. Isolation and feelings of loneliness are growing problems in society; both are indicators that psychological and social health are off balance globally and require attention to return to equilibrium. Lastly, spiritual health focuses on meaning, purpose, and values. It helps us establish peace and harmony in our lives. Spirituality, believing in a force other than ourselves, helps connect us to love within and outside ourselves. Feeling unconditional love within and for those around us is what we can experience when there is balance in our lives. Understanding and appreciating that we are not alone are powerful antidotes to the feelings of loneliness, shame, and disconnection. Connecting with a higher power, the universe, through meditation, prayer, time in nature, reflection, reading, and journaling all help foster a sense of serenity, peacefulness, and calm that help to stabilize and bring balance back into our lives.

Reaching and maintaining balance is a continual process as well as a desired outcome. At times, the balance may be tipped too much in one direction and we will have to find our footing again. Everyone's personal balance will be unique, and the challenge is to be proactive and stay in tune with any changes in our physical, psychological, social, and spiritual health that can impact our overall equilibrium. Stress is a natural part of life and not something that any of us can avoid effectively. Our perception of stress and how we handle it is directly impacted by how grounded or balanced we feel. It is not uncommon to feel overwhelmed by things that other people may deal with easily. The overwhelmed feeling is providing information on the lack of equilibrium in our life. Rather than continue to push ahead and ignore the feelings, it is important to take stock of what is going on, slow down, and build self-awareness. Learning to keep in balance with work, family, and leisure is difficult and needs skillful management of your time. Planning helps, but it also requires setting limits or boundaries.

Some recommendations to optimize balance include the following:

### *Time management*
This involves giving yourself enough time to get things done that are a priority to you, as well as giving yourself permission to slow down. Do you overschedule yourself and are busy "doing" versus "being"? Many people get caught up in busyness in their lives, which externally can seem very appealing, as these people may seem very productive, seem more successful and may potentially be making more money. But at what cost? Without effective time management and balance in our lives, we avoid connecting with ourselves and lose the ability to connect to how we feel and what gives us meaning. We are reactive rather than being proactive. Avoidance of self has a direct relationship with diminished health and wellness.

### *Learning to say "no."*
We all need to regularly evaluate our priorities at work, at home, and elsewhere in an effort to shorten the to-do list and reduce the chances of feeling overwhelmed. Consider delegating activities you don't enjoy or can't handle, and share your concerns and possible solutions with others who can support you. Become aware of your motivation for taking on more tasks; and aware of the challenges in saying "NO." Are you fearful of disapproval? Do you accept tasks out of guilt or a false sense of obligation? Are you concerned what others think of you? The more you say no, the more time you will have to focus on meaningful things in your life.

***Let go of perfectionism***
When we are stressed and have over-extended ourselves, we run the risk of jeopardizing our overall health and wellbeing, which can lead to chronic problems and disease. Acknowledging and accepting our limitations precedes balance as we learn to accept the reality of what is versus what life should be.

**Self-care**
This is the ultimate strategy to achieve and maintain balance in our lives. If we don't take time and steps to preserve our health and well-being, then who will? It is wonderful to have other people in our lives for support, friendship, and to share activities with. However, we are all responsible for ourselves, and we all need to take action for ourselves rather than wait passively for others to take the lead.

What areas in your life feel like they are in balance?

What areas in your life feel out of balance?

What do you need to do to establish balance?

Biologically?

Psychologically?

Socially?

Spiritually?

As represented in the matrix, balance has an observing quality to it when we view it in the second column in partnership with beliefs and boundaries, and it has an observed quality to it when we view it as an outcome from beliefs and boundaries. It is also part of the row of observed qualities that start with acceptance and take us to contentment. If we can accept our limitations in life that can lead to more balance, ultimately, we are on the road to contentment.

Together, beliefs, boundaries, and balance can be experienced as the observing quality (the B column) and are part of the process to connect to the third C column. Individually, beliefs do have an observer quality to them and balance an observed quality, whereas boundaries always have the dynamic observing quality regardless of the perspective one takes on them. Hence, healthy living requires us to have healthy boundaries in context of our vulnerabilities, knowing the risks and adjusting interactions with others such that we deal with our own issues rather than getting enmeshed with other people and their problems.

Balance is also influenced by all qualities in the matrix preceding it. A life oriented around an authentic and passionate purpose is one that is much easier to keep in balance. For this reason, there is no perfect, one-size-fits-all balance plan we need to be striving for. The adage "Life is a journey, not a destination" has much value in terms of reminding us about the value of maintaining a balanced life. The Serenity Prayer, which was discussed earlier, highlights the balance between what we cannot change and what we can, while emphasizing wisdom to know the difference as the observed quality. We all have a choice about how to live our lives, which activities to be involved in, and people to be in relationships with. Try and be cognizant of the signs that your life may be out of balance and continue to take the action needed to regain it!

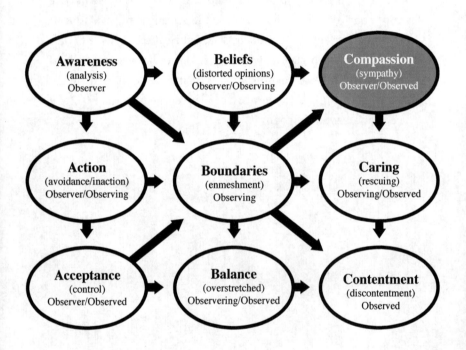

# Chapter 7: Compassion

*"If you want others to be happy, practice compassion.*
*If you want to be happy, practice compassion."*

-Dalai Lama

We live in a challenging time, but we also live in an amazing time full of change. However, change is a process that is often uncomfortable due to the presence of vulnerability and pain related to letting go of people, places, and things we may have become attached to. There are many painful issues threatening to divide us. Political differences, racism, classism, sexism, ageism, stigma, economics, insecurity, and inequality are just a few that are wedging us apart. As we watch the news and get hooked into the sensationalism, as we participate in gossip and get hooked into judgement, as we depend on social media for our sense of worth and value and connection, as we turn to substances and destructive behaviours to escape and avoid our realities, we lose sight of ourselves. We lose sight of the truth, and we become increasingly vulnerable to stress and to negativity in thoughts and emotions that can act as a barrier or obstacle to healthier change.

Negativity and distractions cloud our perspectives and prevent us from noticing what is going well, and from seeing the positives of change that is happening all around us. It is important to remember that we fuel and feed what we focus on. When we focus on the negatives, on our differences, we run the risk of developing and reinforcing a negative world view, and worse, a negative view of ourselves rife with negative self-talk culminating in a dysfunctional/faulty belief system about ourselves and others. One thing most of us can agree upon is that we are all searching for inner peace, for happiness, for contentment. This is commonly misunderstood and referred to as trying to fill the proverbial void within ourselves. We are falsely conditioned to buy, spend, and consume ourselves into filling the emptiness we often feel. What is truly needed are different attitudes about ourselves, and our world. What we need is compassion for each other that involves self-respect and respect for others. This is something that we, the authors of this book, refer to daily in our work with patients as mutual respect and understanding.

Compassion is commonly believed to be sympathy or caring for someone and is often associated with wanting to alleviate the suffering of others. Closer examination of this reveals that as much as that may sound noble, it is not really what compassion truly is, nor is it a noble goal. Alleviation of suffering is a personal journey for each of us that each of us is responsible for, albeit with assistance from professionals and people with lived experience for mutual support. Compassion is better understood in context of having empathy and understanding of both ourselves and others. Compassion is about being a witness to our own suffering while honouring suffering in others without jumping in to fix it. In group psychotherapy, allowing a person in tears to reach for the Kleenex themselves and bearing witness to their emotional pain is an illustration of compassion. It is easy to fall into sympathy or consolation that may make offering the Kleenex to feel like the appropriate response. Consider, though, that offering the Kleenex may distort the message to be, "Don't cry ... don't express feelings ..." Stopping someone else crying may be a fix for one's own discomfort with bearing witness to uncomfortable feelings being expressed. Consoling with "It's going to be all right ..." may feel trite and disingenuous to someone who is experiencing and expressing feelings related to loss that may require time and considerable help to move towards acceptance.

Empathy is about holding unconditional positive regard for others, showing complete support and acceptance no matter what. Sympathy is where we take on the emotions of others as our own. Some people use the analogy of helping someone in a dark hole to explain the difference between sympathy and empathy. The sympathetic responder will get down in the hole with the other person. This effectively means they are both now stuck in the hole, in the darkness, looking for help. The empathetic responder will stay at the top of the hole, offering a helping hand when the other is ready to take it. This person does not get in the hole with them, which may trap both of them. The difference here is boundaries. Empathy is caring with boundaries, as with boundaries, we stay on our side of the street, readily available to offer support that is comfortable to the other, if/when they are ready to ask for it and receive it. Unsolicited support is often perceived to be intrusive and can make the other rebel or withdraw, which has an adverse impact on any relationship that may or may not have been there prior.

Compassion is a motivator that drives us to care for one another, to treat each other with equality, sensitivity, and equanimity, without judgement. In context of our matrix, compassion is the C in the first row, the observed state culminating from the journey through awareness and beliefs. It is also the observer quality that drives caring that leads to our ultimate goal of contentment. Compassion is also an observed dynamic resulting from practicing acceptance and boundaries. As discussed in the chapter on acceptance, we consider compassion to be a spiritual principle, though its effects can be noticed holistically at the biological (physical), psychological (mental and emotional), social, and spiritual levels.

## Biological (Physical Level)

There are many physical benefits to practicing compassion, as psychological well-being results in a healthier physiological functioning. For example, it is well recognized that those who have higher levels of compassion tend to perceive lower levels of stress. Compassion not only greatly reduces our perceptions of stress but reduces its actual overall negative effects on our bodies. It lowers stress for the giver and the receiver. When we are stressed, our bodies produce stress hormones such as cortisol. The more stressed we are, the more we expose our vital organs, bones, joints, muscles, and other tissues to cortisol and other related stress hormones. This has a cumulative effect that alone can "hagger" people over time, effectively causing early onset of any number of physiological health concerns. Many people talk about "compassion fatigue" in care providers, which is in reality "sympathy fatigue," increasing stress in the care provider because of their inability to meet unrealistic standards they may be trying to live up to set by themselves or some external source from which they seek approval and/or fear disapproval.

People with higher levels of self-compassion also tend to be more motivated to take action and undertake health-promoting behaviours on a more routine basis, focusing on progress rather than perfection. There is also the matter of body image. Those with higher levels of self-compassion will tend towards self-acceptance. The relationship between compassion and acceptance is discussed further in the upcoming section on spirituality. Self-acceptance, similar to and in conjunction with self-compassion, means we are less likely to engage in the body-shaming of others, and more importantly the body shaming of ourselves. If our goal truly is to achieve some form of sustainable, lasting contentment, we need to optimize our mind-body relationship by practicing compassion.

## *Psychological (Mental and Emotional Levels)*

The practice of compassion, more specifically self-compassion, is largely a healthy attitude towards our cognitive (thinking) and affective (feeling) well-being. We are emotional and relational beings. As such, we are all driven by our feelings, whether we are consciously aware of them or not. The fastest level whereby we observe and gain information is at the intuitive level. This is commonly referred to as our gut. "What does your gut tell you?" is a common question to connect with our feelings about a person, place, or thing. This happens so fast, and unless we have trained ourselves to notice it right away, we often miss these clear signals. Sometimes we connect to them later on, which leads to more turmoil, especially if we may have agreed to something that is contrary to what we are comfortable with. The next fastest level is the feeling level, which can be complicated and requires time to process. The slowest level is at the level of thought, which can frequently be distorted by expectations that may bear little resemblance to our own feelings and values.

How this is all supposed to work, providing we have a healthy relationship with ourselves, is to observe and gather information through our senses: touch, hearing, vision, taste, and smell. All of these interactions generate feelings that we can observe infants expressing readily, and we all did in our own infancy even though we likely don't remember. We feel the feeling(s) in various parts of our bodies, and the feeling then gets sent to the thought level where relevance and meaning gets attached, based on prior experiences. This interpretation, which is vulnerable to distortion, will often drive our behaviour, the choices we make, and our attitude. This is a highly subconscious process, but with awareness, and the practice of mindfulness, we can become more conscious of it, see where it may be unhealthy. We can then move it towards health through awareness, action, and acceptance, and through awareness to examining beliefs to compassion. Where this process breaks down is when our relationship with ourselves is unhealthy, flawed, or damaged by misperceptions and the cumulative effects over time of unprocessed toxic emotions. This is most often due to the presence and influence of shame.

Shame and guilt are often confused with each other by the untrained observer. Guilt, like stress, is a motivator; we need it, as it helps us to take action. When we do something that goes against our values or beliefs, or the community's values or beliefs, we get the feeling of guilt. It does not feel good, so in theory we are motivated to do it far less or not at all. Guilt can be from not doing something that we know we need to do for ourselves, hence it can serve as a motivator to take action sometimes to release it. Guilt, therefore, is "I feel bad for doing a thing or not doing a thing." Shame is "I am bad." In ourselves-talk, this translates into any number of statements, such as "I'm less than," "I'm not enough," "I'm different," "I have little or no worth or value," "I don't fit in," "I don't belong," etc. Those who are shame-based tend to be unreasonably and at times irrationally hard on themselves and others. Shame also lends itself to perfectionism, which contrary to popular belief is not a virtue, but rather a curse. There is no such thing as perfection, and its pursuit means nothing will ever be good enough, and expectations will seldom, if ever, get met. Shame is simply the most toxic emotion and is extremely corrosive to wellbeing and to a healthy relationships with ourselves and others.

When we combine these internalized shame-based statements with decision-based evidence-making (discussed in the Acceptance chapter), and with FEAR (False Evidence Appearing Real), we get a faulty, fraudulent belief system of self that distorts our perceptions of what is true. We have already made the decision that we are not good enough based on shame, and fear then finds all the reasons this is true. If shame is left unattended to, it has the potential to negatively impact and influence our other belief systems. The way we attend to shame is by practicing self-compassion, and thus connecting to what is true. When working with patients suffering from shame, we tell them that compassion is the antidote to shame. Since it is often unknown to those who suffer from it, shame is externalized or projected out onto others where it is then reflected back to us in the form of perceived judgement. In fact, more often than not, there is no real judgement coming from the other person; it is we who are judging ourselves. Other ways shame manifests itself is through anger.

Anger is sometimes called a secondary emotion because it is the expression of the unrecognized, unresolved feeling underneath the other primary emotions of shame from the past and/ or fear of the future. When we have a shame-based belief system or a shame-based relationship with self, we tend to wear a shame filter. This is like a helmet that we put on, and while wearing it, we touch, taste, smell, see, and hear the world through this helmet, this filter. All incoming and outgoing information is distorted. Another way to express this is that we have a shame button. The more shame we have, the bigger the button. The bigger the button, the more likely that it will get pushed. When the button gets pushed, we get defensive, we get angry, and we engage in conflict, the end result being that we generate more shame.

As therapists, when talking with our patients, we talk in terms of the sad, anxious, impulsive, compulsive brain. We also talk about the addicted brain as having a built-in shame generator so shame is frequently triggered. For no other reason than the way a brain with addiction is wired genetically and then influenced environmentally, it generates shame. With awareness, and with the practice of compassion, we can take the helmet off, and through recovery action we can reduce the size of the button. We can learn to deal with the feelings that arise when the button gets pushed. Rather than talking to ourselves in a negative and counterproductive way that reinforces dysfunction, we learn to talk to ourselves with a nurturing, forgiving, accepting, kind, caring voice. Combined with some engagement in mutual-support programs and psychotherapy to explore and process shame, fear, and anger, we learn to let go, to like ourselves, and we learn to love ourselves. That process brings us more into compassion for ourselves and others around us.

## Social

We are relational beings that exist in a social context. We live in groups, in communities. We crave and need connection, love, affection, friendship, and family. The quality of our relationship with ourselves goes a long way to determining the quality of our relationships with others. We have explored many of the reasons why compassion for self is important in this chapter, but what about compassion for others? As previously discussed, a shame filter can distort our perception of everything around us. It will prevent us from noticing the "little things" in life, from stopping and smelling the roses, as it were. These little things are, in fact, pretty important. A negative belief of self, combined with a negative worldview, will prevent us from noticing what is real, authentic, and beautiful. A shame-based persona will create environments and relationships rife with judgement and expectations. It interferes with being able to see people as they are. It clouds the lens with magical expectations from others and/ or projection of resentments because that is how we may feel: rejected or hard-done-by.

Shame will also manifest most insidiously in the form of passivity. If we don't like ourselves, we need others to like us while still being suspicious if they do. This is due to the nature of self-esteem and self-worth. In the simplest of terms, self-esteem is built with a combination of internal and external validation. When someone has a shame-based relationship with themselves, they are seemingly unable to self or internally validate. This sets them up for the trap of relying on others for validation and self-worth. They seek it out and it can become a drug. Like any good drug, it makes them feel good and they seek it more and more, but it makes them feel artificially good and wears off quick, leaving them with more shame and destructive self-talk.

This sets up the condition or trap of people-pleasing, where we passively put the needs of others ahead of our own needs. We avoid our uncomfortable feelings by stuffing, numbing, and avoiding, until our feelings come out passive-aggressively, which creates conflict in our relationships and ultimately more conflict with ourselves that we may have been trying to deal with by pleasing others. The process of self-shaming is relentless. It is difficult at first, but as we let go of shame through the practice of self-compassion, we gain the capacity to put ourselves and our needs equal to those of others. With compassion, we once again find our right size, our side of the street, we gain the capacity to be assertive, to communicate, think, and feel in a healthier way. As our relationships with ourselves heal, so too do our relationships with others.

### Spiritual

Compassion, as mentioned before, is considered a fundamental spiritual principle or teaching. If you are able to access and practice this principle, then other aspects of spirituality become more accessible, as they exist in the same space, in the same mindset, the same attitudes. Just as unhealthy, uncomfortable emotions such as shame, fear, anger, with related feelings of stress, resentment, regret, judgement, and self-pity all exist in the same space and often conflate together. If you can access one of them, you are in fact vulnerable to all of them, and this is true in both the negative and positive directions. There is an old proverb that states you cannot be in self-pity and gratitude at the same time. Self-pity means wallowing in despair, feeling sorry for ourselves, usually connected with mourning the loss of something we had (indicating the presence of shame), or something we perceive we will never get (indicating the presence of fear). Gratitude is being okay with what we have, the feeling that something or someone is enough. The proverb is indeed a gauntlet challenge, meaning if you have awareness, and recognize you are in an attitude of self-pity and have a genuine desire to shift yourself out of it, doing some work to shift your attention to what you do have, what is going well, will shift you into an attitude of gratitude and away from self-pity. This gauntlet challenge can also be applied to shame and self-compassion. They simply cannot exist in the same space. Increase in one decreases the other.

The point we are making is we cannot be in two places at the same time, and this applies to our mindset as well. If we recognize we are experiencing unhealthy self-talk or uncomfortable feelings, we can change the tone and energy of ourselves-talk, we can move through uncomfortable feelings and get to the other side more quickly by practicing these spiritual principles. Compassion prevents getting stuck in judgement (shame) and allows for patience, tolerance, understanding, and empathy to take hold, to move us towards acceptance and serenity, which is the antidote to shame. It allows us to shift from beating ourselves up. Compassion helps us to realize we need and deserve to cut ourselves some slack, to lighten up on ourselves, to accept and forgive ourselves for our flaws and imperfections. Practicing faith allows us to move through fear, and in many cases, prevents fear from taking hold. Faith allows trust in ourselves and our ability to adapt to unknown situations. Practicing faith increases our capacity to access and practice other principles such as humility. Just as focusing on the negatives creates a downward spiral, focusing on healthier initiatives, on our relationship with a higher power, creates and promotes health in an upwardly mobile direction. This does not mean avoidance or ignoring; rather, it means acceptance of the undesirable (what we don't want or don't have), while highlighting the desirable (what we have and what we may truly want). Interestingly, even desirable and undesirable can change when our perspectives change!

### *Putting Compassion into Practice*

Throughout this chapter, we have alluded to ways we can practice compassion and why it is an important practice on our journey towards contentment. We talked about practicing empathy versus sympathy and the importance of caring with boundaries. We talked about challenging our negative self-talk, which is based on faulty information, based on shame, with compassion, which allows us to connect to what is true, kind, gentle, and fair. Compassion is about connection and is therefore best practiced with others as this will help us to practice it on ourselves. This means reaching out, getting vulnerable, and sharing our common human experiences. Courage is another spiritual principle that allows us to be vulnerable. Courage requires action despite fear. Compassion helps us to suspend judgement of ourselves and others. In an ideal world, we simply would not compare ourselves to others. If we do, it is far healthier to compare our similarities than our differences. Comparing how we are alike will build bridges, whereas comparing how we are not will create chasms between us.

Practicing affirmations is another way to practice self-compassion. When a person with a shame-based view of themselves says, "Affirmations are stupid and they do not work," as therapists, we remind them that they do work but require a shift in perspective. The evidence is clear, as negatively affirming your-self for years makes you believe those affirmations: "I'm stupid, I'm not enough, I don't have worth or value," etc. We must chal-lenge negative, unhealthy affirmations and program ourselves with new, healthy ones. If unhealthy thought patterns are deeply entrenched, we may not be able to eradicate the unhealthy pat-terns, but we can learn to disengage and refocus on dealing with these patterns with surrender and acceptance.

Random acts of kindness are another way we can practice compassion. If we are doing these acts seeking approval, this will feed our egos/grandiosity, which is the opposite of humil-ity. Volunteerism is another way we can practice compassion, by freely giving of self with no thought of reward. These actions, practiced with humility, means no one will know we've done these things but us and our higher power, and that's okay. In fact, action with humility is desirable, it feels good, and it will give way to much-needed self-validation and a happier, healthier relationship with ourselves and others.

*Explore.* How have you looked at compassion in the past?

How much self-compassion do you practice?

What can you do to practice more self-compassion?

What can you do to practice more compassion towards others?

Reviewing the first row of the matrix, we have proposed that as awareness moves into the process of becoming more concrete, it gives rise to our beliefs. Beliefs can be fixed or fluid, and the lens through which everything filters in our life. The chapter on beliefs explored this in more detail, in context of the observer quality and the observing quality. If beliefs become fixed, then the natural flow to compassion in the first row would be hampered.

Compassion is a natural expression or observed quality of awareness through beliefs. It refers to the appreciation of diversity such that we can look beyond ourselves and appreciate the experiences and perspectives of others without judgment, without attaching a right or wrong value to them. Compassion can also become an internalized value that then has an observer quality to it such that our interactions with others and the environment are governed by this meaningful ethic. True caring, as will be discussed further in the next chapter, is dependent on compassion and boundaries. Compassion as an observer quality then translates into contentment through caring!

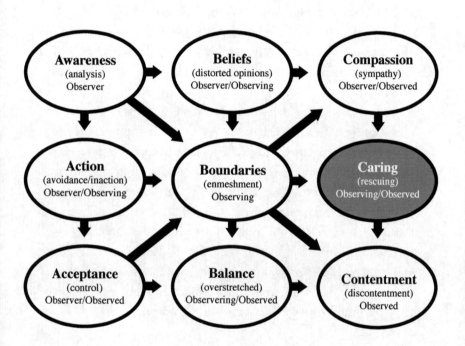

# Chapter 8: Caring

*"Nurturing is not complex. It's simply being tuned in to the thing or person before you and offering small gestures toward what it needs at that time."*

-Mary Anne Radmacher

Caring can be defined as an adjective, verb, and noun. When we look at the matrix, as we move from action to boundaries, the outcome is caring. Caring is described from the observed perspective. Here, caring is defined as a noun and adjective. As a noun, it is the provision of what is necessary for the health, wellness, and protection of someone or something, and as an adjective, it is used as a descriptor word such as helpful and kind. When we look at caring from a verb perspective, this is the observing action/process direction of the matrix. Compassion as the observer quality, through caring as the observing capacity, results in the observed outcome of contentment. Here, caring is defined as a verb as taking action to demonstrate care for someone or something.

Caring for ourselves is central to staying well. Action and boundaries are necessary components that result in the outcome of caring. Caring for ourselves is always necessary before we can care for anyone else. Think of the adage and reminder when you are flying: "You have to put your own oxygen mask on first before assisting others." The reason you are instructed to do this by the flight attendant is because you will not be able to help anyone else with their mask if you run out of your own oxygen supply. It makes sense, right? But so many people feel challenged in caring for themselves first. The most common hang-up is "it is selfish." This is not true. This will be emphasized again: NOT true. Taking care of ourselves first is necessary and fundamental. We will not have the capacity to care for anyone else authentically if we don't. It is our responsibility to notice our own pain and fatigue and to take appropriate action to take care of ourselves before turning to care for others.

Caring for yourself isn't always a comfortable and cozy process. It is about doing things that appear hard because of your past experiences with social conditioning. Compassion for yourself and others motivates that drive to care for one another. It is fundamental to start with yourself first. Each of us, as an individual, is the foundation of the equation. If you are not connected to yourself, you are vulnerable to sympathy, projection, and rescuing others in an attempt to seek relief from your own feelings that you may or may not be fully aware of.

### Empathy vs. Sympathy

As discussed, compassion is having empathy and understanding both for ourselves and others. Empathy does not mean agreement with another person's thoughts and feelings. It is the maintenance of neutrality and non-judgemental, unconditional, positive regard for others. It is caring with boundaries, because with boundaries, we stay on our side of the street. This doesn't mean that feelings are not experienced about what is happening on the other side. What it means is that there is self-awareness and no action is taken to seek relief, escape, or reward by engaging with the other side of the street.

For example, when you have started to take action and explore your health in a holistic manner, some of your friends may start poking fun at you. This may hurt your feelings. You may decide to be assertive in talking with them if they are receptive or you may decide to explore boundaries further and limit your exposure to these friends. You may stop calling, texting, and reaching out until there is some evidence of change in them. However, you may feel more hurt if it seems that they do not even notice your absence from their lives and do not make any attempts to connect.

In sympathy, we begin to feel sorry for ourselves and fall into the trap of self-pity. An unhealthy action in this example would be to cross onto their side of the street and reach out to those "friends" to look for some sort of rationale as to why they haven't called you. This action is relief-seeking and is not a caring action for yourself. A caring action would be to journal about your feelings, having empathy for yourself. This would be to acknowledge without judgement your feelings and maintain boundaries. As you lean into your pain and the hurt you are feeling, you are in the observing state of caring, resulting in a release of your emotional pain, in contrast to staying stuck in seeking relief and feeling more pain.

Empathy and sympathy also occur in the context of other people. As mentioned, empathy is caring with boundaries. Sympathy, on the other hand, lacks boundaries, as there you take on other people's emotions as if they were your own. It often feels like pity for the other, but it really is enmeshment. By staying on your side of the street, it is essential to be aware of your own emotional reactions to the other side of the street. Now what do you do with your feelings? In sympathy, you end up joining the other person in their pain, projecting your own painful experiences into the mix. Although it may look like you are connecting with the other person, it is largely commiseration and takes away from the authenticity and genuineness of the connection. The motivation often becomes more about you than the other person. Many times, a person receiving sympathy, which can sound like "I am so sorry you are going through this," feels like they are being pitied. It can cause a shutdown in healthy communication. When you are feeling pity when listening to someone else, you are in a place of projecting your own feelings onto the other person.

In empathy, we listen to understand the other person's experience in a caring manner. It becomes important to ask questions and offer statements showing we are listening such as "That sounds very hard for you, am I hearing you right?" You hold space for yourself and the other individual. You pay attention to your own feelings that come up. You are in a place of caring for you first, which in turn provides you with the capacity to care for the other person.

*Explore.* Practice empathy within yourself by journaling your thoughts and feelings and take note of the following:

Can you listen without judgement to your feelings?

What judgements and stereotypes do come up?
Are there certain labels you place on yourself?
What are your foundational beliefs about yourself, family, friendship, love, sex, success, relationships?
Are these your beliefs, or are they beliefs that have been passed down onto you that you have assumed as your own?

Practice empathetic and active listening with another person. Questions and statements to draw upon are:

How does that feel for you?
Tell me more about that.
That sounds (insert feeling word) for you, am I hearing you right?
Paraphrase: So, what I am hearing is ... is that right?

Pay attention to your own emotional reactions. Remain neutral without projecting your own personal stereotypes and biases.

What did you learn from this exercise?

## *Helping vs Rescuing*

Helping and rescuing can look the same on the surface. However, the motivation behind these actions is very different. Developing more self-awareness, in context of other windows of the matrix as we have discussed, is key to distinguishing between the two. Helping also comes from a place of taking your own action and having boundaries. When you are healthily connected to yourself, feelings, and values, you have the capacity to help others.

When helping others, it is important to consider first and foremost: is the other person even asking for help? If help is being requested, remember your own self- compassion. This means you need to consider your own feelings first before responding.

*Explore.* Explore the following questions:
Are you in a position to help the other person?
Do you have the resources to help (e.g., time and energy)?
Is helping in line with your own values?
What feelings come up for you in their request of help?

If the other individual is not asking for your help, then pay attention to your own feelings that are coming up in observing them in status quo. Offering unsolicited help leaves you vulnerable to projecting your own feelings onto the other person. In turn, your offer of help is self-motivated. This means it is about your own relief-seeking of the discomfort you are experiencing. It can be hard to witness someone struggling. Rescuing can come from many places. As an example, it can come from a place of fear or even a place of annoyance.

When rescuing another individual, you rob them of the opportunity of learning and growing from their own life experience. By jumping in, you interfere with their growth and development and reinforce the message that you don't feel the person is capable of doing it themselves. This doesn't sound very caring, doesn't it? Although it may not be your intention, it is a consequence of rescuing.

*Explore.* Explore the following questions:

How are you feeling watching this person?
What memories does this trigger in you?
What feelings are coming up for you?
What is your motivation in offering "help"?
What is the real/true issue?

What boundaries do you need for yourself? (e.g., internal boundary of not offering help unless it is directly asked for, or an external boundary of how much exposure you have with the person).

A key distinction between helping and rescuing is the motivation behind it. Simply put, are you trying to fix or problem-solve? Are you attached to an outcome? Attachment to an outcome can vary. Commonly, a person may ask you for your opinion on what to do. You may feel consciously detached from an outcome. After sharing your opinion, you find out the person did something different than your suggestion or perhaps they did nothing at all. You feel agitated and ask yourself, "Why did they even bother asking me if they weren't going to do it?" This agitation is information that you were attached to an outcome of the individual doing what you suggested. This offer of help comes from a place of control, which is connected to rescuing, problem-solving, or fixing. Sometimes this can occur at a subconscious level and you will not know until after the fact. This is ok! This is the opportunity to invite compassion and in turn care for yourself and process feelings that have been triggered from a subconscious place. This is how growth happens.

Another way that you can be attached to an outcome is in someone's response (or lack thereof) to your help. Are you looking for an accolade for your help? Are you expecting the other person to do the same for you in future? This is reward-driven, where your offer of help has strings attached to it. An assumption may be made that you are banking your help (rescue) with an expectation that you can call upon this person and they will return the favor. Have you found yourself in a place of judging the other person for their lack of reaction? "They didn't even say thank you or give credit to me for helping!" This shows that you had an attachment to some form of approval or validation from the other person.

*Explore.* Explore the following questions:

Are you carrying any expectations of offering help?
Are you attached to any outcomes?
What is your motivation in helping?

True helping comes from a place of caring for yourself and others. It comes from a place where many parts of the matrix come together: awareness, beliefs, compassion, action, boundaries, acceptance, and balance. You can see how all elements flow together in every which direction as feelings are explored in each section. The more connected you are to your holistic action (self-care) and boundaries, the outcome of caring is reinforced. Oftentimes you may look back at challenging experiences and have some gratitude leading into the ultimate state of contentment. In the moment you may not have felt that way, but with time and space you can see how these challenges have happened for you rather than happened to you.

Through action and boundaries, you can be in the observed state of caring while also discovering through compassion the observing state of caring. These moments have led you to the place of caring for yourself, and in turn having the capacity to authentically care for others. Remember, caring for yourself is essential and necessary in order to genuinely care for others.

*Explore.* In what ways do you care for yourself?

What action can you take for yourself that is caring?

Are there places in your life where you feel overwhelmed, frustrated, or depleted? What boundaries do you need for yourself?

What caring self-talk do you practice for yourself?

Develop some affirmations/mantras to recite to yourself on a daily basis.

Reviewing the second row of the matrix, we have explored action, boundaries, and caring. Action by its nature represents a process of change, activity, and progress. In order to truly understand or appreciate something, exploration is required. This represents movement or dynamism. We know intuitively and explicitly that everything within us and around us is in constant motion. Although awareness can be appreciated as encompassing all there is, it still requires some action to appreciate the manifestations (observed). The second row represents the observing quality of process, from action to boundaries to caring, as they display aspects of some dynamism/action. Caring does have a more observed quality, being in the third column, whereas boundaries are always dynamic in context of what may or may not be happening. The chapter on action explored how we can focus on action in harmony with life rather than action that can create more confusion and dysfunction.

Boundaries represent the recognition of the strength of separateness. For each of us to be our optimum, we need to have clarity of who we are and what we need as individuals to remain healthy. If a boundary is not clear, then we can have a negative impact on others around us by doing things that are not ours to do, while neglecting what we need to do ourselves. This common problem wreaks havoc in relationships, families, and communities around the world. The chapter on boundaries explored the process of setting and maintaining boundaries that may need to shift and evolve throughout our lifetime. Boundaries require growing and expanding awareness, guided by the manifestation of contentment, to keep us going in healthy directions in our lives with caring.

Caring is the manifestation of healthy action with boundaries, yet caring needs to be appreciated on an ongoing basis as a process or observing quality. Caring for yourself is central to staying well. This chapter on caring explored both the observed part of caring as well as the observing part of caring. We have to consistently remember that caring for ourselves is always necessary before we can care for anyone else.

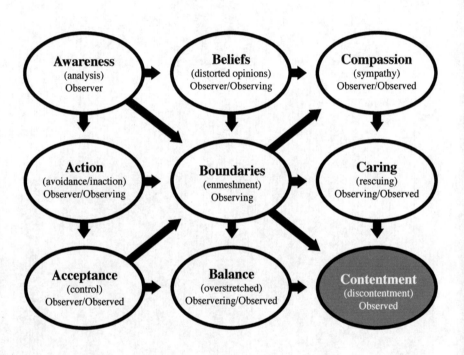

# Chapter 9: Contentment

*"Contentment is the greatest form of wealth."*
*Acharya Nagarjuna*

We live in a human-constructed world that at times goes against what we were biologically, psychologically, socially, and spiritually designed for more naturally. We were not meant to live in concrete towers. We were not destined to work more than we play. We did not always need money in order to get our basic needs met. We were not designed to live alone in isolation and disconnection. Our anthropological history tells us that we hunted and gathered together for a few hours each day in order to meet our individual and our community's basic needs. We then spent the remaining hours of the day building relationships with ourselves and each other. We are designed bio-psycho-social-spiritually to follow our natural curiosity, to explore and discover what it is that makes us tick, what our passions are, what brings us pleasure and joy. Procreation, ensuring the survival of our species, has been a common theme for most of us that gets translated often into perpetuation of our family lineage. Most of us have other passions and pursuits as well, such as the arts, music, science, healing, education, caregiving, construction, public service, and leadership. No matter what our calling or our political leanings, no matter our race, gender, sex, ethnicity, or age, we're all looking for the same thing. We are looking for sustainable, lasting contentment day to day and as we reflect back on our lives or look towards the future.

Contentment can be defined in many ways. In 1943, psychologist Abraham Maslow, while likely borrowing from North American Indigenous culture, became famous for crafting Maslow's Hierarchy of Needs. It is a pyramid structure that ranks our human needs from basic/physiological, to safety/security, to love/belonging, to esteem/self-worth. At the top of the pyramid is self-actualization, which is simply a fancy term for personal growth or inner peace, a feeling or condition of lasting and sustainable overall contentment. Contentment does not mean we aren't driven to excel, that we don't want more out of life, but it does mean there is an absence of perfectionism, of unrealistic expectations, and in many cases the absence altogether of expectations. In the realm of minimalism, there exists the statement that less is more. This refers to having gratitude for what we have versus the greed-driven pursuit of more. If we can be content in our own skin in any given moment, then time for ourselves becomes a gift to be appreciated and fully realized, and there is no longer such a thing as boredom or wanting to fix whatever may be making us uncomfortable. Who among us doesn't long to be happy and to experience joy more consistently? Too often happiness and joy happen only by accident; they are seemingly fleeting conditions that come and go. Our dysfunctional, human-constructed world has even normalized turning to the use of harmful substances, most notably alcohol, in an attempt to artificially obtain and rise to this condition. Here again, even the substance, and even in the destructive behaviour users are just trying to find some semblance of inner peace and escape. The condition of contentment holds us in this space, without employing some external means to get there or stay there. It is contentment itself that most people truly seek when they say they just want to be happy.

As stated in the introduction of this book, contentment is the ultimate observed quality that arises from the journey through awareness, action, acceptance, beliefs, boundaries, balance, compassion, and caring. As we've explored, there are short and long roads to contentment. The phrase "We get out of the experience what we put into the experience" applies. That being said, the longer road will often lead to longer-lasting conditions of contentment.

As contentment is the end goal and last window in our matrix, with awareness as the beginning, let's go back to awareness for a bit. There is an old phrase, "You can't fix it if you don't know it's broken." The implication here isn't that we are broken; rather, it simply means we need some level of knowledge and understanding—we need to be observers if we are going to make changes. Being content with ourselves and our surroundings cannot be based on avoidance, ignorance, or inaction. It does not mean complacency. In fact, to live in a state of lasting contentment as much as possible requires us to practice a high degree of self-monitoring that is a composite of awareness, action, and acceptance, beliefs, boundaries, and balance through compassion and caring. It requires insight, self-awareness, and expansion of our consciousness. This is the beginning of true connection to self and the rest of our universe, something that many of us struggle with. It is this connection to ourselves and all there is that is so critically important to finding true contentment. When we lose sight of ourselves and our place in the universe, we become disconnected. We forget to ask our self-important questions such as "How am I feeling?" "What do I want and need?" "Who am I?" Contentment doesn't make uncomfortable feelings go away, but it gives us stability and opportunity to deal with them so we can move through them and stay on our journey of personal growth.

Once again, there are several paths we can take through the matrix. The quickest route to contentment from awareness is diagonally through boundaries. If we chose to follow the longer, more sustainable path that travels through the "A" words, then our next window is action. One of the hardest things to do is to take action on something. There are many feelings that clog up the works and keep us stuck; feelings such as shame, guilt, fear, anger, and resentment. We get stuck looking at and focusing on the total sum of all the parts of whatever lies in front of us, often overwhelmed by our feelings and by the pressure and expectations we or someone else has placed upon us. We are less likely to get stuck in uncomfortable feelings, and we are less likely to be connected to outcomes, if we keep our focus on willingness, balanced actions, and staying in process. If we're feeling restless, irritable, discontent (aka itchy, bitchy, twitchy), we're more likely to be avoidant, to wait until motivation and willingness come. If we're not careful, we could be waiting for a long time. Often, we simply need to take a leap of faith, take the action, even with the smallest amount of willingness—the motivation will come later. We all need validation of process to have confidence in something working or being meaningful, but it is essential to focus more on process rather than how quickly one can get to desirable outcome(s).

As mentioned above, there are many feelings that can be serious obstacles to obtaining a state of contentment. These feelings are a blend of what has come before, what is happening now, and what might happen in the future. Exploring and practicing acceptance of what is beyond our control is an important part of the journey towards contentment. Tools such as the Serenity Prayer that help us recognize where we are powerless, where we need to surrender control and let go, help us move towards acceptance. The relationship between acceptance and contentment is such that if we are able to do one, we are able to do the other, as these are conditions that exist in the same mind space. Accepting what comes, what is, and disconnecting from attachment to outcomes goes a long way to minimizing frustration and disappointment, feelings that contribute to being discontent.

Our journey through the "B" column begins with checking in with our beliefs. One of the hardest things to do is to challenge our beliefs. These are often entrenched ways of seeing ourselves and our world. They are shaped by our observations of not what is necessarily true, but largely what we believe is true. The immediate antecedents to contentment are boundaries, caring, and balance. These emphasize the need to channel awareness, action, acceptance, beliefs, and compassion such that these antecedents are reinforced. Contentment arises from the creation and reinforcement of congruence, alignment with our awareness, beliefs, and values that are part of the preceding windows in our matrix. This is the central part of the spiritual process, a cultivation of an attitude that recognizes that all things are happening *for* me versus happening *to* me. When we are content and connected, behaving towards ourselves and others in a way that is true to our genuine authentic self, we are more likely to maintain that shift in our perspective, to be a part of something instead of the centre of it all, which can actually be very isolating.

Can you imagine a world where everyone acted as if they were the centre of it all? Perhaps so many problems in our world arise from trying to control everyone through one ideology. Contentment is an individual process that arises from within rather than being imposed from outside by the pursuit and acquisition of material wealth. The overall rise in the standard of living around the world over the last few centuries has not resulted in higher levels of contentment. The little mountain country of Bhutan has tried to popularize the concept of GNH— Gross National Happiness—as the true measure of sustainability for humans on planet Earth rather than GNP—Gross National Product—which measures more material growth. Countries around the world that are doing well on a lot of health and healthy public policy measures are the ones where there is more equitable wealth distribution and provision of basic services for all, rather than countries where the wealth is more concentrated. For example, the United States of America ranks poorly on many sociological indices despite ranking at the top level for material wealth; a reminder that lack of balance, caring, and boundaries has a very visible negative impact on the population as a whole.

As explored in the chapter on boundaries, they are for you and adhered to by you and are not up to other people to respect and honour. Only we can honour and respect our own boundaries, which then sends a clear message to those around us, increasing the likelihood for personal contentment, which has the potential then to spread to others. The observed state of contentment is inextricably linked to the flow of the observing process of caring, as it is to the observer qualities of compassion. We can be satisfied and clear for ourselves, sustaining our needs regardless of how people react to our boundaries. Gratitude enters in for the opportunity of new learning and information gathering. Contentment will say, "If others respect my boundary, great! If others do not respect or understand my boundary, that's okay! It is all just information about the other person." Contentment and gratitude allow feelings to move through us rather than holding them hostage, the most direct outcome through awareness and boundaries moving diagonally in the matrix.

When resistance is felt, contentment can vanish quickly, while agitation, irritation, and frustration arise. The focus moves from connection to our own being to projecting and blaming those around us. Control will start to bubble up, and energy will be spent on what others are or aren't doing. We can fall prey to trying to figure out how to manipulate others to "make them" respect our boundaries. At times, control may be more covert and manifest in the form of avoidance. All of the feelings that are being experienced get stuffed down and put away. However, the impact and weight stay with us and comes to the surface as discontentment. This idea is well known in twelve-step recovery circles, where people support each other through these hard-to-pin-down feelings that are collectively summarized as restless, irritable, and discontent. The disease of addiction is easily activated in those situations, taking an individual towards seeking a fix through reward, relief, or escape.

We hope that everyone connects with contentment as a natural outcome of connecting to balance holistically in our life. As the chapter on balance explains, it isn't a one-size-fits-all formula. Balance is unique to each of us. It is not a destination, meaning it is not something that we get to or achieve; it is something we strive for daily in process with life's ups and downs. Contentment is experienced when we can embrace the fluidity of life. Stress occurs externally and internally as a natural process of our inter-actions with ourselves and others. Every day some things go smoothly, especially if they are predictable and familiar, whereas others don't, especially if they are unfamiliar and unpredictable. Contentment provides us the space of the observed perspective and really allows us to see through an open lens of flexibility with balance, boundaries, and caring. This viewpoint affords us the ability to collect information if an imbalance or dysfunction is being experienced. With that information, it then guides us to restore balance, which naturally brings contentment. We don't have to strive for contentment. In fact, striving for contentment without balance, boundaries, and caring will bring more frustra-tion and strife. It is important to have no judgement of ourselves or others regardless of balance or imbalance, with compassion and caring to take us to the outcome of contentment. We can culti-vate curiosity, appreciation, and gratitude for the opportunity of reflecting, new learning, and insight, staying in the process with a sense of detachment, which is another feature of contentment.

One of the most well-known passages from a Vedic text, the Bhagavad Gita, Chapter 2, verse 47, says that we must focus on action in accord with our *dharma* (duty) without attachment to the results or fruits of the actions; further, not only must we not be attached to the fruits of the actions, but we cannot be attached to inaction.

Discontentment will invariably surface when judgement and expectations are experienced with respect to the experience of imbalance. Remember, balance is just a dynamic, a moment in present time. It is an outcome of clarity in beliefs and boundaries, intricately linked to the degree of acceptance of all that is. Frustration results from expectations and the assumption, "I have arrived at the state of balance, and I should stay the same" Simply put, life is ever-moving and constantly changing. Contentment provides us with the observed ability to ride the waves of life.

*Consider exploring:*

What feelings are coming up for you as you consider contentment?

Where are you feeling drained or stretched too thin—is there a lack of balance?

What boundaries are you lacking or missing?

What is working for you?

What isn't working for you?

What feelings come up when connecting with gratitude for new learning?

The result of contentment in the C column of the matrix is experienced as you stay in the process of caring for yourself and connecting with others in a caring, interdependent manner, while detaching from any outcome. You can be truly connected to your own feelings and maintain self-awareness that caring is coming from a healthy place, rather than self-serving motives. This is a genuine definition of mutual support. Regardless of what the other person does or does not do, if you are in this place of caring, feelings will come and go, and contentment will naturally prevail. Contentment does not make you void of feelings (even the uncomfortable ones!); rather, it allows you to welcome them in and in turn release them. There is no labelling of your feelings as good or bad, right or wrong—they remain as information providers in their own ebbs and flows.

If caring becomes rescuing, discontentment will arise as information related to problems with boundaries. You may find that you consciously feel that you are not attached to an outcome or have any expectations of what the other person does or doesn't do, yet something in you feels uncomfortable while interacting with others. Discontentment bubbling can be a reminder to review that you are not trying to rescue others or expecting them to rescue you at some level. Accepting these feelings for what they are—information—brings you back to the place of contentment pretty effortlessly with detachment from the expectations.

*Consider exploring:*

When uncomfortable feelings come up for you, what are they? What do they say?

Who triggers rescuing vs. supporting? What feelings come up for you?

How can you practice detaching with love?

Compassion is having empathy and understanding both for yourself and the other person. Compassion is experienced in both the observer and observed state. You will note that compassion occurs for yourself, with yourself. Without this connection to self, you do not have the capacity to have authentic compassion for others. Contentment arises when compassion is experienced both as the observer and observed as it creates the ability to truly be present, connected, self-aware, and in the flow of conversation.

Discontentment will surface and provide information that the ego and self-will/self-judgement is being imposed. The whole C column—compassion, caring and contentment—becomes self-reinforcing as you gain confidence from the observer qualities of the A column and observing qualities of the B column. Similarly, contentment becomes self-reinforcing with acceptance and balance in the third row of observed, as the confidence builds from the observer qualities of the first row and the observing qualities of the second row.

*Consider exploring:*

How do you practice compassion for yourself when discontentment arises?

How do you show compassion for others?

What does compassion feel like from the seat of contentment?

What does acceptance for all that is feel like?

What feelings are associated with having balance in your life?

Contentment from the observed perspective, regardless of which window of the matrix you are in, places you in the seat of gratitude, allowing you to flow with the process rather than control and dictate the process. It welcomes all feelings in, without judgement, without expectation, without labels. Feelings aren't an indicator of success, as one may misguidedly expect if constantly striving for happiness; rather, they are a compass to navigate the world with acceptance and compassion, balance and caring, with boundaries—consistent action in context of clarity in beliefs. It is a true connection to spirituality, letting go of any outcomes and trusting in the process. Your job is to collect the information from the observer, stay in the process of observing, and in turn experience the observed perspective. It is not a destination that is arrived at, but rather a symptom of being present, curious, connected, and open, enjoying the dance of life!

*Consider exploring:*

What does contentment feel like to you?

What does discontentment feel like to you?

What self-care tools help you connect to your feelings?

How do you connect to the present moment?

Practice meditation—observing thoughts and feelings as they come and float away.

Contentment, being the ultimate observed quality, is virtually guaranteed if we stay in the process with the other aspects of the living matrix framework discussed in this book. Contentment can be experienced through feelings of gratitude for what one has even in the face of loss and/or deprivation, which is a reminder of attachment, often considered the root cause of suffering.

We wish you lots of self-reflection in our matrix framework and continued growth with awareness, boundaries, and contentment. Namaste!

# Epilogue

We have been using the concepts discussed in this book pretty consistently for over ten years. We have also shared them in an organized week-long program at HUM in the last couple of years. Below are some reflections and personal experiences in using the matrix concepts as applied in real life by our patients/clients at HUM.

*I wake with a start. My heart pounds in preparation for flight, or a fight! I don't know where I am. I don't recognize the vast expanse of trees dusted with snow surrounding me. I'm in the back seat of a truck full of strangers and it is screeching to a halt behind another truck which has launched off a snowbank into the ditch. There are no landmarks, there is no context for this moment. I don't know where I am, but thanks to recovery ... I'm not lost. Thanks to the choices I make in recovery, I am waking up from a nap after an honest day's work in a truck driving to the airport after shift change so that I can fly home to my family for my two weeks off. Thanks to recovery, I am not the one who drove that truck we are stopping to look at into the ditch. Waking up, I didn't know where I was, but I did know who I was. Ironically, in addiction I always knew where I was, but I was perpetually lost.*

*For all the benefits that awareness has helped me uncover, in my experience, awareness can also be a harsh mistress. Firstly, it floated me to the surface of the quagmire that was my life in addiction. Once there, I became aware of how years of rationalization, escape, and avoidance had led me to a very unhealthy place. I became aware of feelings that I had taken great pains to avoid and the severe discomfort that I was in. The good news is, once awareness became part of my consciousness, I wanted to do something; to take action to improve my situation and restore my life's balance. Living in recovery, I am aware. Because of this I accept the past, I accept who I am, and I make decisions today that align with my beliefs and newfound boundaries. Today I can experience contentment rather than the experience of endlessly chasing it. Today I am grateful for my recovery and the challenges that addiction put(s) in my path.*

Gordon


*The ABC matrix begins where I started in my recovery journey, with awareness. I knew I was feeling discouraged, tired, resentful, and out of balance in my life. Some relationships were difficult. I attempted to feel safe by controlling and rescuing others. I was willing to try something different and take action on change. This matrix lays out the path towards contentment.*

*For me, it was a process of acknowledging and accepting my feelings and becoming aware of my unhelpful thoughts and behaviours. This brought me to clarity about what was healthy and safe for me in my life and in my relationships, and into the crucial centre of the matrix-boundaries. I have been able to communicate my boundaries with compassion and respect for myself and others. I no longer feel stuck in old patterns and there is a sense of freedom and contentment.*

*Now, when unmanageability pops up in my life, the ABC matrix gives me insight as to where things have gone off the rails and has given me a process for getting things back on track to contentment.*

Nancy

*I've been invited to share my experience with the 3x3 matrix framework. The most relatable for me to this experience is the movie The Matrix. Morpheus reveals the truth to Neo, and Neo's blind pane suddenly becomes Awareness. This was also my experience. Believing my life existed in a certain plane of existence to suddenly be abruptly smacked into Awareness.*

*The first of what would be the start of many moments of awareness began when I suddenly became aware of my emotions (how I feel) and the deepest truth about my relationship (dysfunction) with my mother. I guess upon reflection I can give myself some credit that even before this moment I existed in some basic state of the observer (intuition), feeling like something was "off" or uncomfortable within my life. From the state of awareness, there are so many paths towards contentment, and in my experience, the path is not linear.*

*It was suggested to me to have an immediate boundary with my relationship with my mother to address the lifelong enmeshment I have had with her. I will be honest that this boundary of "no contact" immediately challenged my belief system. I was raised on the belief that a son honours his mother and father. This singular belief challenged not only my earthly relationships but also my spiritual ones. The shame of choosing what was a healthy action and boundary for myself pushed right up against this deeply embedded "being a good son" belief. It even made me question my own worth to a Higher Power (GOD). But as I stayed in the process by talking with my recovery network, journaling, and meditating, I found a sense of acceptance and contentment about who I am, what I need, and my worthiness. After all, it's my life, and I am responsible for my own mental health and emotional state of being. Currently, I am working in the realm of compassion and caring, first with myself, then with my family and primary relationships. I hope to further my contentment and acceptance of life through these two vectors.*

*Awareness now is starting to become simpler. It really is a moment of reflection upon which I become aware of how I feel, or what I want or need. From there I have a healthy group of recovery humans and professionals that are the crucible in which I can further refine my wants and needs. Sometimes, it is abundantly clear what information my emotional state is saying, and I can move towards taking action, challenging my beliefs (the lens through which I view life), or implementing a boundary for myself. This is the fun part, figuring out what works for you. There is no right or wrong way: this is something I've learned and want to share with you. This black-and-white thinking continues to be a vulnerability for me, which I am learning to let go of (beliefs). I wish you, the reader, well on your journey of awareness (Ayurved) and hope we cross paths in the Ayur (lifespan). Namaste.*

Justin

*I grew up with the belief that seeking relief and avoiding feelings was how I would feel contentment. I acted as if the obliteration of self through drugs, alcohol, relationships, and sex would open a door to an awareness of self that would allow me to feel connected to myself and others. It was, of course, the exact opposite. The chaos it created in my life obscured the boundaries that would have supported my needs and instead I was left seeking relief from the cravings that always seemed slightly out of reach. It was as if contentment was waiting for me on the other side of intoxication and if I could just do it "right," I would arrive. The irony is that the feelings and awareness of self that I was avoiding was the door I had to walk through to find true contentment.*

*For me, awareness of feelings is so important to my recovery. I used to try to think my way through my feelings and sometimes still do. I used analysis to mask my feelings, attribute motives to my actions, and prop up my self-esteem. But because I was unaware of my actual feelings, my motives were concealed from me, and my self-esteem was based on a lie.*

*If I wanted to move towards true contentment, and I did, I needed to take different action. First, I started outing all the thoughts and feelings that were floating around in my head. And as I unpacked everything in group therapy, I started gaining awareness around what was my truth and what was not my truth. I started separating out the feelings that were generated by the disease, mostly shame and fear, and the feelings that were more me. By having a place that I felt safe enough to explore my feelings, I was able to grow my awareness of my feelings, which supported exploring more feelings. It is a positive-feedback loop, awareness supporting action that supports a growing awareness.*

*And as I dug deeper into my feelings and outed them to the other participants in group therapy, I noticed I started feeling less shame around them and more acceptance. The acceptance was important for me because if I could acknowledge how I truly felt, then I could start internalizing beliefs that honoured those feelings. For example, I started to shift my belief that feelings were a sign of weakness and to be avoided instead of acknowledged. And once I was more capable of acknowledging my feelings, I was better equipped to see what experiences, people, and places were triggering the addict-y feelings of shame and fear, and I could start to create healthy boundaries around those exposures.*

*A common trap for me in relationships that triggered the disease is a belief that I needed to honour them because of the past we shared. But by acknowledging those feelings, I was able to put in place healthy boundaries that supported a more emotionally balanced life. It doesn't mean I never saw those people again, because that isn't balance either, but it did mean that perhaps I saw them less or I made sure to see them in a context that was more supportive of my recovery. In hindsight, I see this now as being more caring of myself and showing myself more compassion. I was honouring my own feelings and my own needs instead of putting my perceptions of what I thought were the needs of others ahead of my own.*

*Compassion isn't pity or sympathy; it is a recognition that all of us as humans deserve to have our needs met. For me personally, it meant acknowledging that my feelings and needs were valid and that I could live a life that was aligned with my feelings and needs, and as it turns out, when I live in this way, I get to experience contentment. Contentment in this case is the outcome of acknowledging I am enough in this moment. That my feelings and needs don't need to be changed, just acknowledged and honoured. This is the gift of recovery.*

Ian

*Awareness and action to acceptance—my disease loves analysis—thinking and digging. It was a way of life for me before recovery and I didn't realize it. I've been practicing hearing and letting go of analysis and moving towards watching, listening, and building awareness. I try to listen to my intuition and heart instead of my head.*

*My disease also loves just floating along in life and not taking ownership. Reflecting on what I can do in my life helps me hear my voice, and then I can go from victim to survivor. I have to be careful not to focus on solutions/fixing but rather being in the process and seeing what information my intuition and higher power give me. At times this feel extremely confusing, so I need internal boundaries around the disease and compassion for myself. This is hard stuff to practice.*

*When I'm able to be aware and take action, I find acceptance. Acceptance feels like surrender and allows me to be in the cycle again—aware, action, acceptance. I may not like a situation, but I can accept it.*

*Acceptance to balance to contentment. Balance is finding the middle path. My disease tends to keep me overly busy and distracted, so I've been mindful of not overbooking myself and cancelling plans if my disease gets active or I want time alone. Putting myself first can be challenging.*

*Contentment feels peaceful to me. When I take space for myself with self-care, like walking, yoga, or meditation, I find that I'm better able to find gratitude in my life regardless of what's happening. Contentment doesn't mean the lack of feelings or things are perfect; to me it means I'm safe and calm watching what's happening.*

Allison

# Appendix A

## *Contemplation, Concentration, Meditation*

Meditation is a word that means different things to different people. Many people think it is a hard thing to do. Many think they have to clear their minds, which is impossible to do consistently for any of us. Many people think meditation is something you can only do when you are less stressed out. In fact, none of these assertions are valid. Meditation is really a technique for connecting with yourself. All the things out there called "meditation" attempt to go in that direction. However, it is helpful to know what these different things are so you can connect with yourself the best way possible.

Consider that our inner experience is what life is really all about. The external world that we interact with through our senses generates internal impressions, memories, thoughts, and feelings that determine how we behave towards ourselves and others. Our society gives a lot of importance to thought and right thinking. Hence, what many people call meditation is really contemplation: that could mean reading something meaningful to gain perspective on one's life, such as reading scripture or inspirational materials, as is common for a lot of people. In Alcoholics Anonymous literature and practice, people talk about increasing their conscious connection to "God as we understood Him" through prayer and meditation. Often people say that prayer is asking for help and meditation is listening. That listening is in many ways to ourselves, our higher consciousness and connection to all there is in the universe. This is usually not easy to do, and much more happens along the way.

These days what is typically called meditation is actually concentration, where you focus on something to help centre and relax yourself. Mindfulness or focusing on the present is very popular, and a great technique for slowing down and letting go of the attachment to the burdens of the past or fears of the future. It takes practice and has great benefit. There are other ways you can do this—focusing on breath, progressive muscle relaxation, visualization, and guided imagery—that are all techniques to get away from the turmoil in your mind with thoughts and feelings. All of these techniques help get you to a state of relaxation, with the hope that regular practice will make you calmer. People use these techniques with various degrees of success. Some use them only for rescue, as needed. They work better if they become part of your routine, as using something when only seeking relief can make matters worse; we are all less efficient and less able to follow through on our commitments to ourselves when stressed out. What about connection to higher consciousness in concentration techniques? This happens at all times, but how conscious you are of it really varies. It is more likely to happen when you are relaxed and not ruminating over or trying to control the turmoil that may be happening in your mind.

The states of consciousness that we are all familiar with are sleeping, dreaming, and waking. As much as we don't truly understand the function of sleeping and dreaming, we do know that they are essential parts of being healthy. A good night's sleep often goes a long way towards reframing and providing perspective on what may have been a huge burden the day before. Whether we remember our dreams or not, they do serve a function that is measurable. Sleep studies can show us whether we are entering into dream states, which our brain needs nightly. We know that recreational drugs and many medications disrupt natural sleep architecture, largely by disrupting REM (rapid eye movement) or dreaming.

So, are there more states of consciousness? The unequivocal answer is YES! You can research what they are, but for our purposes, consider that there is a state that we all experience from time to time when everything is exactly as it is supposed to be, and you are in the flow. People usually experience this when in good company, out in nature, or engaging in some activity that they are passionate about or proficient at, when things are happening naturally without much effort. This is what meditation truly is, and it works more effectively if we have a technique to do that regularly. That technique that we, the authors, use is Transcendental Meditation ™.

Meditation is the experience of letting go of trying to do anything, trying to fix anything, trying to analyze or even understand. Meditation is spontaneous and does require staying in process without judgment of good or bad. It is something one may experience at times when using contemplation or concentration techniques.

# Appendix B

## *The Matrix Reflections in the 12 Steps\**

The 12 Steps of Alcoholics Anonymous (AA) were conceptualized in the USA in the 1930s. There was a deliberate distinction made away from religion (prescriptive) to an open concept of spirituality through "God as we understood Him." As much as there is no direct evidence of the founders of AA adopting this idea from the East, it is the most central idea in the Ved, the ancient Indian paradigm that encapsulates all knowledge—that we have to explore and follow our own dharma, life purpose, or duty, rather than someone else's, thus outlining the personal nature of each person's existence, regardless of their background or challenges they may face.

In the observer, observing, observed paradigm, dharma is the observer state of awareness, followed by karma (action), which is the observing state, leading to phala (fruits), the results of the action that are consequences to one following or not following one's dharma, highlighting the surrender aspects of what one needs in life. The first three steps that are as follows thus reflect the trinity, yet together Steps One, Two, and Three define the foundation or awareness to move one to action that is part of Steps Four, Five, Six, Seven, Eight, and Nine. Steps Four, Five, Six, Seven, Eight, and Nine can be organized as pairs, such as Four/Five, Six/Seven, Eight/Nine or as a trinity, like Four/Five/

Six and Seven/Eight/Nine to illustrate the robustness of the matrix paradigm. Similarly, Steps Ten, Eleven, and Twelve, taken together, reflect the acceptance that is the result of the previous steps.

1. We admitted we were powerless over our addiction, that our lives had become unmanageable.

2. We came to believe that a Power greater than ourselves could restore us to sanity.

3. We made a decision to turn our will and our lives over to the care of God as we understood Him.

The recognition of powerlessness and unmanageability is central to awareness, before one can move to the action—believing that there is a higher power that can potentially help—to turning it over to that higher power through acceptance. This awareness-action-acceptance through Steps One, Two, and Three is often referred to as the foundation for further progress through the steps, which enhances awareness and serves as the awareness to the action steps, which are Steps Four/Five, Six/Seven, Eight/Nine as awareness, action, and acceptance in the Matrix for Life.

Steps One, Two, and Three can also be viewed as the top row: awareness, beliefs, and compassion. Step Two requires a fundamental shift in believing in a Higher Power. The surrender that is reflected in Step Three is a compassionate act related to acceptance of the realities of life.

*as modified by Narcotics Anonymous

4. We made a searching and fearless moral inventory of ourselves.

5. We admitted to God, to ourselves, and to another human being the exact nature of our wrongs.

Considerable work is required to look at oneself in the above steps, usually with the help of a sponsor and peer support from other individuals in recovery to enhance once awareness within the action steps. Hence, they connect back to growth in awareness, which is reflected on a daily basis in Step 10.

6. We were entirely ready to have God remove all these defects of character.

7. We humbly asked Him to remove our shortcomings.

This is the true action of connecting with God or one's own understanding of one's higher power. As much as it uses language of "defects of character," it is really vulnerabilities or "shortcomings" that one is asking to be removed. As one stays in the process, the clarity comes that this is an ongoing process rather than an event. This connection with one's higher power is a reminder regarding boundaries, meaning what is within one's own domain of influence—internally and externally—and what is not, thus it being left up to whatever concept of God or higher power one may have.

8. We made a list of all persons we had harmed and became willing to make amends to them all.

9. We made direct amends to such people wherever possible, except when to do so would injure them or others.

This step is the culmination of the process begun in Steps Four/Five, getting to the result through Steps Six/Seven. It is the acknowledgement of the "amends" that are needed for the harm that occurred through the disease. Some misinterpret these as apologies. The important process, though, is ownership of reality—what happened and what is needed now on an ongoing basis—rather than looking for absolution or forgiveness. Steps Eight/Nine also reflect the caring for oneself and others. The making of amends and acceptance of what happened, in context of what is different now, leads one naturally to acceptance, balance, and contentment.

One could look at the first three steps in context of the first row of the matrix: awareness, beliefs, and compassion. Steps Four/Five, Six/Seven, and Eight/Nine can be seen as the second row, action, boundaries, and caring, and the third row as acceptance, balance, and contentment connects with Steps Ten, Eleven, and Twelve.

10.  We continued to take personal inventory, and when we were wrong, promptly admitted it.

11.  We sought through prayer and meditation to improve our conscious contact with God as we understood Him, praying only for knowledge of His will for us and the power to carry that out.

12.  Having had a spiritual awakening as the result of these steps, we tried to carry this message to addicts, and to practice these principles in all our affairs.

Steps Ten, Eleven, and Twelve, taken separately, represent the observer, observing, and observed, whereas taken together, they are the outcome or observed, leading to contentment, as they reflect acceptance and balance in context of awareness and spiritual connection.

Thus, one can appreciate the reflection of ancient knowledge that is part of the Twelve Steps, which is a reminder that everything is connected, even when a direct reference may not be made or be evident. Personal reflection is needed for all personal growth, in determining one's own dharma—duty or direction in life—rather than following someone else's or getting bogged down in intellectual analysis. The Matrix for Life is meant to be experienced at a feeling and spiritual level more than the thinking level.